FELTING

Elvira López Del Prado Rivas

4880 Lower Valley Road • Atglen, PA 19310

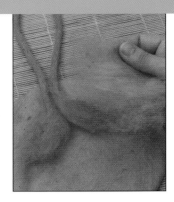

Other Schiffer Books by the Author:
Costume Jewelry.
ISBN: 978-0-7643-4149-6

Other Schiffer Books on Related Subjects:
Felt, Fiber, and Stone: Creative Jewelry Designs & Techniques.
ISBN: 978-0-7643-3668-3

Fun Felt Crafts: Penny Rugs & Pretty Things from Recycled Wool.
ISBN: 978-0-7643-3299-9

Making Simple Felted Jewelry.
ISBN: 978-0-7643-3570-9

Published by Schiffer Publishing, Ltd.
4880 Lower Valley Road
Atglen, PA 19310
Phone: (610) 593-1777; Fax: (610) 593-2002
E-mail: Info@schifferbooks.com

For our complete selection of fine books on this and related subjects, please visit our website at **www.schifferbooks.com.** You may also write for a free catalog.

This book may be purchased from the publisher. Please try your bookstore first.

We are always looking for people to write books on new and related subjects. If you have an idea for a book, please contact us at **proposals@schifferbooks.com.**

Schiffer Publishing's titles are available at special discounts for bulk purchases for sales promotions or premiums. Special editions, including personalized covers, corporate imprints, and excerpts can be created in large quantities for special needs. For more information, contact the publisher.

FELTING

Contents

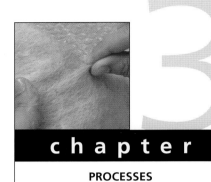

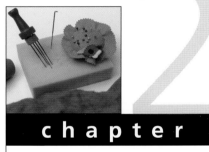

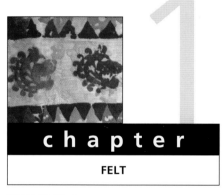

chapter

TECHNIQUES

chapter

PROJECTS

Introduction

The purpose of this book is to resolve all the potential doubts that may emerge as you begin your first project with felt. Indeed, the intention is for you to become familiar with the great range of possibilities that felt has to offer. Amongst the unique projects found in these pages, you will encounter challenges that, although both interesting and diverse, can be easily recreated with a little enthusiasm and a touch of creativity. To better understand the processes involved in creating with felt, it is first necessary to understand its origin and its uses throughout history, as well as to take a look at new and up-to-date uses for this material. All this is explained in the first chapter.

In the following two chapters, the tools needed for making felt are introduced, as are the most common materials used when working with it. There is also a description of the processes involved, from the moment the wool is first obtained to those that come later. There is also an extensive chapter which explains, step by step, various projects made with felt. In turn, this chapter is divided into three sections: one dedicated to felt projects for children to enjoy, another to decorating the home, and lastly to using your creativity freely to create an array of accessories. All the projects are presented in ascending order of difficulty, using the various techniques and types of felt available.

The book ends with an interesting gallery of pictures of pieces created by artists from all over the world, giving you a chance to appreciate the wide range of possibilities offered by the medium of felt.

Elvira López del Prado Rivas
Jewelry and Costume Jewelry Designer

1 Felt

In recent times, the world of arts and crafts has witnessed the resurgence of an age-old material well-known to artisans all over the world: felt.

Used since the Bronze Age, felt has evolved to become one of humankind's most unique forms of expression due to its physical and chemical characteristics, and these are particularly appreciated by visual artists.

By learning about the origins of felt, it will be much easier to understand the qualities and behavior of this material.

What is felt?

This is the first question that arises when discussing this material. The answer is simple: felt is wool. Its most important characteristic is that it is not the result of intersecting warp (threads running lengthwise in a woven fabric) and weft (horizontal threads woven crossways in a woven fabric). Therefore, felt differs from other fabrics in that it is not a woven fabric at all.

Moreover, felt is the most ancient textile in the world. With felt, wool fibers mesh together through a process that will be explained later, forming a tight, even fabric made entirely of proteins of animal origin. This is the fabric we refer to as felt.

Origins

Legend has it that Noah placed wool from his sheep on the floor of the Ark to make the journey more comfortable for the animals. When the animals disembarked, Noah saw that the wool, having grown wet and matted during the journey, had compressed into a compact fabric. This legend is in fact just one of many to mark the supposedly first appearance of felt cloth to humankind. In reality, however, the discovery of felt was probably coincidental.

Nomadic Asiatic cultures mastered its fabrication, as it formed an essential element for the survival of their family groups. They used felt to build the yurts or tent-like structures in which they lived, which, in spite of their thickness, were light and therefore easy to transport from place to place.

The domestication of sheep has its origin in Mesopotamia between 8000 and 9000 B.C., when the shepherds discovered that these animals were more useful as a source of wool than as food.

In archaeological sites from this area, pieces of felt have been discovered dating back to the Bronze Age from approximately 3500 B.C. Today, these and similarly well-conserved pieces can be found in the National Museum of Denmark (Nationalmuseet) in Copenhagen as well as in the Hermitage in Saint Petersburg, Russia (in which pieces of felt from the Pazyryk culture are conserved). The Pazyryk culture originated on the Russian steppes; its peoples were descendants of the Scythians, a semi-nomadic tribe from present day Iran.

Swan, made from felt, 12" high. Pazyryk Culture, 4th-5th centuries B.C., Russia. Hermitage Museum, Saint Petersburg, Russia.

Fragment of carpet made from felt, 55" x 40", from the Altai Region, Russia. 5th century B.C., Attributed to the Pazyryk Culture. Hermitage Museum, St. Petersburg, Russia.

Fragment of carpet made from felt, 250" x 180", from the Altai Region, Russia. 4th-5th centuries B.C., Attributed to the Pazyryk Culture. Hermitage Museum, St. Petersburg, Russia.

Illustration showing nomadic Asiatic cultures and the typical Mongol tents made of felt called yurts.

Properties and characteristics

Wool is the most sophisticated and complex of all fibers; it is endlessly recyclable and its organic structure is able to recognize even small changes in the environment, allowing it to react and keep the sheep comfortable.

Wool, as a fiber, is formed of two main parts: the cuticle and the cortex. About 10% of the fiber is the cuticle, the layer around the actual fiber that repels moisture, created from scale-like cells that vary according to the species of sheep.

The cortex constitutes the remaining 90% of the fiber, and it is this which gives wool its resistance and elasticity; it is able to absorb up to 30% of its weight—much more than that any other fiber.

The cortex has a bilateral structure formed by the orthocortex and the paracortex, which occur in different proportions, depending on the type of wool.

This structural ratio determines the amount of curl in the fiber.

Wool fiber has some unique physical properties that differentiate it from all other fibers.

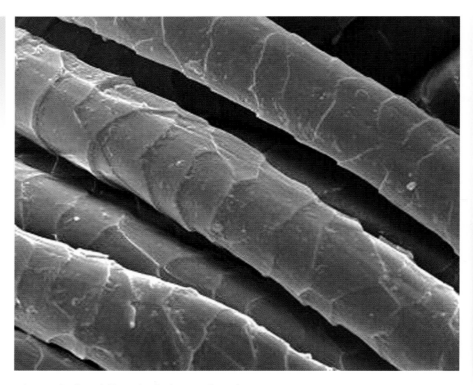

Micrograph of wool fibers clearly showing the scales.

For example, a noticeable difference is the fineness of wool; its fibers can vary in diameter from 50 microns to less than 2 microns, but they can measure up to 12" in length, depending on the species.

Woolen fibers are hygroscopic, or readily able to absorb moisture from the atmosphere and yet lose it in a drier atmosphere. Among other qualities, wool fibers constitute a material which is warm, lustrous, elastic, and flexible. It is also insulating, fire-resistant, and absorbs sound.

Scale drawing of a Merino wool fiber. In this diagram, the darkest section corresponds to the orthocortex of the Merino wool fiber.

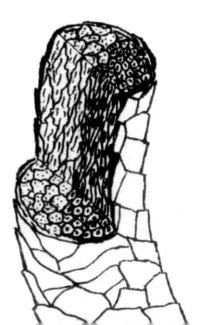

MOHAIR

BLACKFACE

Examples of the orthocortex and paracortex in Mohair woolen fibers (Angora goat) and in Scottish Blackface (wool sheep).

ORTHO-CORTEX

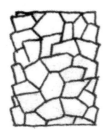

PARA-CORTEX

Traditional uses

Recently, the use of felt has enjoyed a resurgence. Traditionally, this material has been used in very diverse areas: for rugs, hats, jackets and coats, felt-tip markers, tennis balls, filters for vacuum cleaners and air conditioning units, and also for polishing disks for machinery, amongst many other uses.

In reality, wool is not limited to being used separately. On occasion, its fibers are mixed with other fibers, such as vegetable fibers like cotton, ramie, and jute to achieve different finishes. Wool is also used with synthetic fibers, like nylon. These blends are used to create a felt which is either thicker or lighter, depending on its intended purpose.

Chalkboard eraser with felt base.

Traditional felt hat.

Felt tennis balls.

Billiards table. Traditionally, the cover is made of felt.

Coat made from felt.

Marker pen with felt interior.

Rediscovering felt

Today, there are many objects made of felt; simply by taking a look around any craft market, you will find a great variety of ideas to inspire you.

Thanks to the work of artisans around the world who have continuously worked to improve felting techniques, leading to an unending spread of new inspirations and discoveries, much has been learned about pieces that, in the past, were especially difficult to make.

Here, you can see some of the objects that can be found on display in stores as well as some other examples of artists' creativity with felt.

Children's book made from sheets of felt.

Felt covered glass. Ana Rodríguez, Spain.

Bag made entirely from felt.

Children's "Mezzmerizzing" felt doll. Inger Maaike Lutje Schipholt, Netherlands.

Felt and silk shawl. Created using the nuno technique by Spanish artist Mercè Puig.

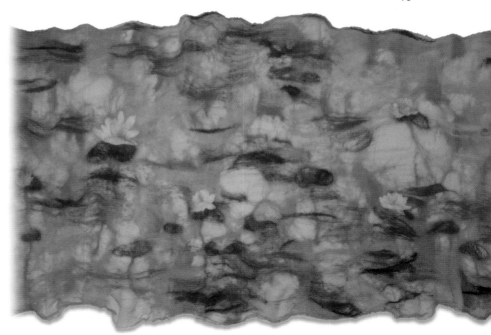

Hair clips made from felt. Ana Rodriguez, Spain.

Men's felt house slippers.

Sweet Dreams T-Shirt made from felt. Joana Juhe Corbalán, Spain.

Fascinator, to be worn with a wedding gown. Cristina Vázquez, Spain.

chapter

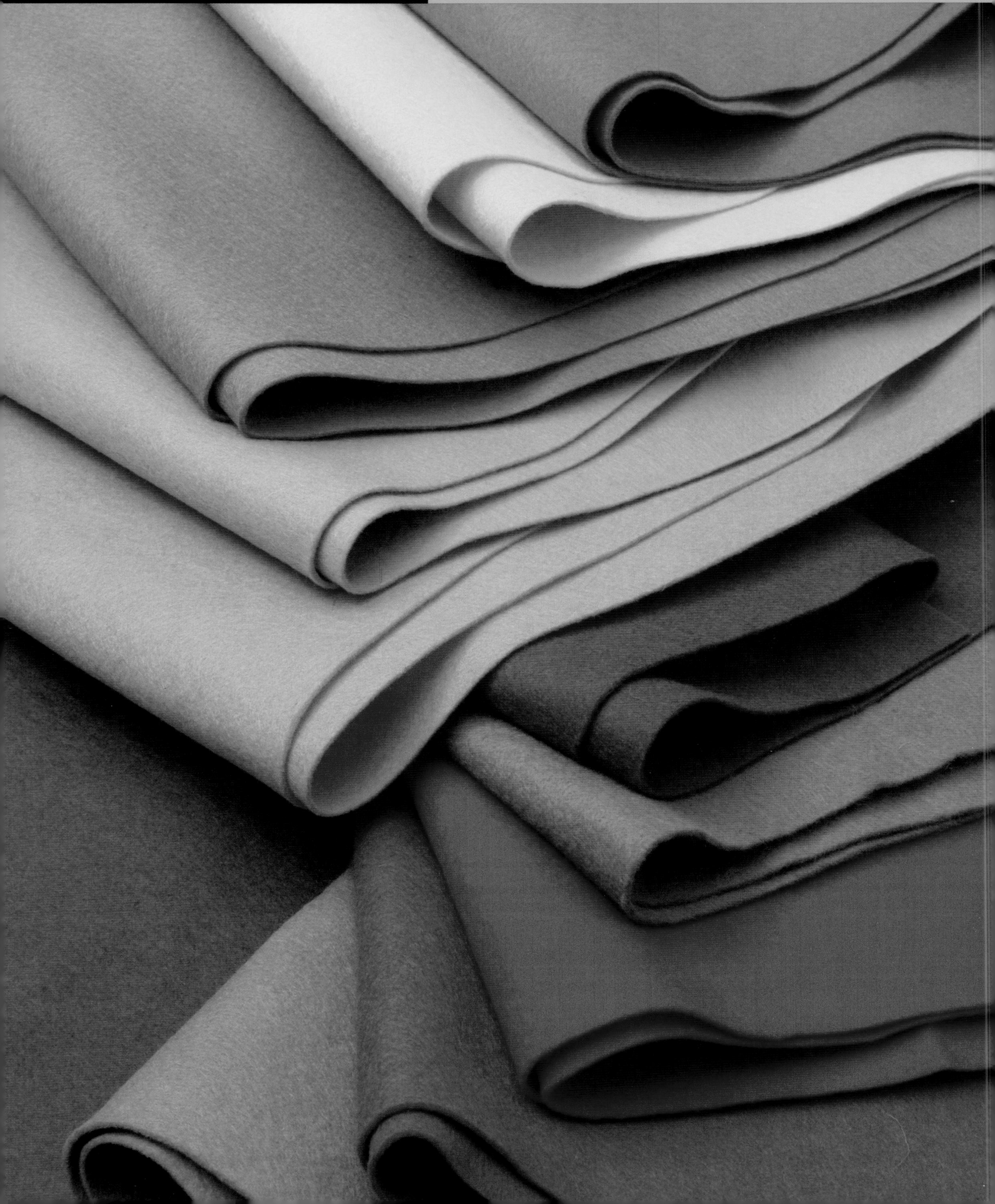

Materials and tools

This chapter will introduce you to all the materials that can be used for felting wool. You will see the different ways of using felt and its various decorative uses, as well as glues, special soaps, and more.

In terms of tools, the subject is even more extensive; apart from those specifically designed for making felt, there are a great many everyday items that can be used for this purpose.

Materials and tools

Wool can be found in many formats and colors. This section shows you those which are best suited to felting, as well as some supplementary materials that will make the job even easier. The tools used have been divided into three main groups according to the method of felting they are used for: wet felting, dry felting, and flat felt.

The last group gathers together the materials and supplementary tools which will be used in specific projects.

Materials

In order to start working with felt, it is not necessary to assemble lots of different materials, as all you really need is a modest selection of wool in varying colors, sizes, and formats. This may include sheets of commercially produced felt sold in different weights and colors; combed wool; carded wool; skeins of wool and an assortment of mild soaps.

In the last part of this section, you will see some of the additional materials that are used as supplementary tools when working with felt: textile adhesives, instant glues, sewing threads, silks, and gauzes, which will be needed for felting using the nuno technique.

Main materials

The essential material for making felt is wool. Its quality and characteristics differ according to the breed of the sheep that it originates from. The treatment given to the wool after shearing is also important. If it has been carded, it usually becomes a little coarser, whilst if it has been combed it becomes smoother and more delicate against the skin. The type of wool chosen will depend on the project at hand.

You will also work with sheets of commercially produced felt. These are used for various projects, occasionally even being combined with felting wools.

Commercially produced 0.25-inch-thick sheets of felt.

• Felt sheets

Felt sheets come in an extensive range of colors and weights, the most common of which are 0.25" and 1 mm thick. Before you buy, make sure that they are 100% wool, as some fabrics and interlinings are made of synthetic materials which are difficult to use for the projects described in this book. One of felt's unique qualities is that it does not fray, meaning that

Combed and dyed Merino wool.

Various 1-mm-thick sheets of felt.

Carded dyed wool.

Skeins of dyed and natural wool of different types.

it does not need hemming. It can be found in arts and craft stores as well as haberdashery and specialist stores.

• Combed merino wool

This wool has been combed to compare the fibers, with only the longest being selected in order to make the wool more flexible and improve its quality. It has a silky, lustrous texture which feels especially pleasant to the touch. These characteristics make Merino wool especially suitable for making accessories such as hats, scarves, and the like.

• Carded Tyrol wool

This wool is coarser because it has only been carded and not had its fibers sorted. As a result, Tyrol wool is extremely easy to felt and is often used for home furnishings and projects which require tough felt such as rugs, slippers, and the like.

• Balls of wool

All types of woolen yarn can be made into felt if they are made of 100% wool and have not been treated to make them into washable yarns, meaning that they will not shrink when washed in the washing machine.

• Mild soap

The soap used should be mild with no additives and a neutral pH level. Whether using a bar or flakes, it must always be combined with hot water—approximately 104°F (40°C), or whatever your hands can tolerate.

If opting for soap flakes, dissolve them in hot water at a ratio of 0.05kg/l, or two tablespoons of soap per liter of water.

Bars of soap should be used directly on the wool or for lathering your hands. If felting in a washing machine, you should use the same soap you would normally use.

Bar of mild soap and soap flakes.

Fabric glue and cyanoacrylate instant glue.

Silk and gauze fabrics.

Supplementary materials

Supplementary materials such as fabric glues, instant glues, silks, and gauzes all help you to work with felt.

There are also additional materials which are useful when working on specific projects; the list of these is never ending, limited only by your inventiveness when using everyday items in novel ways to create your own particular pieces.

• Glues

In certain projects, it is advisable to use two different types of glue: one type of glue is sometimes needed for slow-contact fabric drying, while a second type is occasionally needed for quick-drying and must be applied with caution.

• Silks and gauzes

Silks and gauzes are needed when using the nuno technique, which consists of felting wool over a very lightweight, loose fabric. This allows the fibers to penetrate the silk in order for felting to take place and results in the creation of felt with very unique textures.

Besides silk or gauze, there are a great variety of sheer fabrics that are suitable for this type of felting. These fabrics are sold in specialist stores.

Additional materials

In this section you will find an assortment of materials that will be used for future projects. They are not necessarily felting materials in their own right, but they will serve to add the final touches to many of the pieces in the book, and you can gradually add to the list when start creating your own projects.

Such materials include offcuts and remnants of felt sheets, wadding and filler, water soluble Vilene (water-soluble interfacing that dissolves in cold water, also known as Soluvlies or Solufleece), tailor's chalk, cords, wire, crimp beads and brooch backs (traditionally used in costume jewelry making), varnish, latex-based acrylic paint, polystyrene balls, and self-adhesive magnetic paper. All these materials can be found in specialist art supplies stores and in haberdashery and hardware stores.

A) Offcuts from felt sheets; B) wadding and filler; C) water soluble Vilene; D) tailor's chalk; E) rocaille beads; F) metal lamp base; G) nylon thread; H) cord; I) copper wire; J) crimp beads; K) brooch backs; L) varnish; M) latex-based acrylic paint; N) polystyrene balls of various sizes; O) self-adhesive magnetic paper.

Tools

The tools used to create and work with felt are very diverse, and need to be adapted according to the projects undertaken and skills required.

In addition to the specialist tools available for working with wool, you can also use everyday household items if the need arises, as it is not always possible to have the right tools at hand. Each artisan will favor certain tools over others and use them in his or her own way.

Next you will be introduced to the tools that will be used for the exercises in this book: those used for wet felting and those used for dry felting (including flat felt), as well as those used in both processes.

Tools for wet felting

In this section, you will be shown some of the many everyday tools that you will find easily in stores that sells household goods and furnishings, such as towels, bowls and trays, paint brushes, nylon fabric, bubble wrap, containers from canned foods or cosmetics, rollers, rubber bands, bamboo mats, polystyrene heads, knitting needles, brushes, sponges, and a washing machine.

• Sponges and brushes

These are used to dampen the wool before beginning the felting process. Using any type of sponge, even a bath sponge, will prevent the entire workspace from getting wet. Brushes are employed in a similar way, or in some cases you can just use your hands to dampen the wool. Any brush can be used; for the projects in this book a kitchen brush will be used.

• Knitting needles

Knitting needles are used to weave together balls of yarn, which will then be felted by hand or in the washing machine. There are different types of needles: the traditional knitting needles, circular needles, and double-pointed needles. They are made of wood or plastic and can be adapted to all types of projects, depending on the artisan's individual level of skill.

• Polystyrene head

This serves as a base when creating hats and caps from felt and is useful for shaping the material into the desired shape. They can also be made from plastic or wood, and you can find them in specialist arts and crafts stores.

• Bamboo mat

These come in a variety of different sizes and are sold in homeware stores. Used together with the roller, the small sticks help to smooth out the wool in the final fulling process.

• Rubber bands

These bands can be made of rubber, flexible silicone, or any other elastic material. They are placed around the bamboo mat to prevent the felt inside from shifting during rolling.

• Broomsticks and wooden and plastic rollers

These are useful for rolling up felt. As a result the wool fibers mesh and come together to form a compact piece of felt. Any long stick without edges can be used for rolling; for example, a wooden roller, a broomstick, or a plastic tube, depending on the requirements of the project.

Bamboo mat.

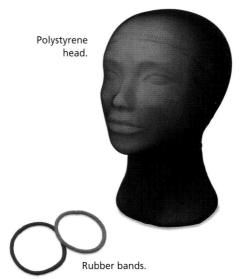
Polystyrene head.

Rubber bands.

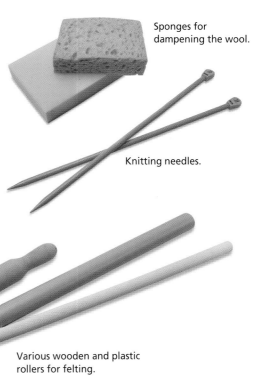
Sponges for dampening the wool.

Knitting needles.

Various wooden and plastic rollers for felting.

Jelly jars and cosmetics pots.

Bath and hand towels.

Nylon mesh fabric and plastic bubble wrap.

Bowl, tray, and brush for dampening wool.

• Containers and cork mats

Containers such as jelly jars and cosmetic canisters are useful as molds for felting; cork coasters and mats are also useful for craftwork.

• Towels

You can use any bath or hand towel to prevent the rollers from moving as you work, and also to soak up any excess water from the piece.

• Bubble wrap, plastic gloves, and nylon mesh fabric

Plastic facilitates the massaging of the wool in the first part of the felting process. This massaging can be done with or without the use of gloves or plastic bags on your hands, depending on the piece and your level of skill. The plastic bubbles are placed in contact with the felt, or underneath it with the bubbles facing upwards. In this case, the nylon fabric is arranged over the felt to prevent the colors of the wool from bleeding when massaged.

• Bowls and trays

These are used for keeping the hot water in during felting. You can also use the trays for the cold water during the final rinse. Any other similar container can be used for keeping water in.

• Washing machine

The washing machine is used for felting projects that involve knitted woolen yarn and knitting needles. The water should be at a temperature between 104°F and 140°F (40°C – 60°C); choose a short wash cycle, as 20 minutes is enough to felt the piece, and use your usual washing powder. It is a good idea to put an old item of clothing, or a pair of slippers that you do not use, into the washing machine, as giving the fabric something to rub against facilitates the felting process.

Tools for dry felting

The dry felting process for handcrafted pieces requires very few tools: felting needles, which are sold in various sizes, as well as foam felting pads, which are found in different materials and thicknesses.

• Individual felting needles

The three most common sizes of needle—small, medium, and large—are characterized by the thickness of their tips. The largest felts more but also leaves more holes in the felt. The medium-sized needle is the most frequently used, as it felts quickly and leaves less marks. Lastly, there is the small needle, which felts very slowly and is used for carrying out small areas and detailed work.

• Felting needles with handle

These are the same felting needles as those described above, but they are fixed to a handle. There are many different models, depending on the manufacturer; the most common have four needles but some have more. They are used to felt large areas of wool.

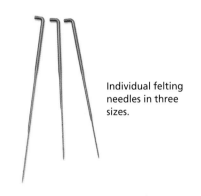

Individual felting needles in three sizes.

Felting needles with handle.

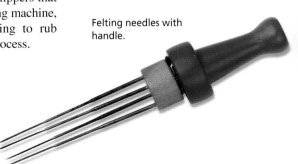

Foam felting pad and EVA foam.

• **Scissors**

Sharp scissors are ideal for cutting fabric. If you need to make a very precise cut, a rotary cutter with a handle can be used.

• **Needles, pins, and thread**

To work with flat felt, you need a wide choice of colored thread, as many pieces need to be sewn by machine or by hand. You also need a good selection of sewing needles and pins to hold the material in place as you work.

Various colored sewing threads, sewing needles, and pins.

Additional tools

Here is a selection of other tools that will be useful for the felting exercises in this book, which can be used with all felting techniques.

These can be added to when necessary: pinking shears (for cutting flat felt), some toothpicks, a metal punch, an iron, some metal cutters (used in working with polymer clay, rubber stamps, and cutting pliers and round-nose pliers (used for jewelry making). All these tools can be found in specialist arts and crafts stores.

Tape measure.

Scissors.

• **Foam felting pads**

These are found in many thicknesses and sizes; you can also use EVA foam which is more durable and less bulky, and can be especially useful for some pieces.

It is essential to use a base of this type when using felting needles; otherwise the tips of the needles will break. Foam pads come in many different forms, depending on the manufacturer.

Tools for flat felt

The tools used to work with flat felt are the same as those used for working with fabric: for example, a sewing machine (which requires some basic knowledge), a tape measure or ruler, scissors or a rotary blade cutter for precision cutting, sewing needles and threads, and a pen or marker for making templates or for using on the felt itself. You can find these materials in specialist fabric stores.

Whilst the book groups these tools together as those specifically used with flat felt, these tools can also be used in other techniques. They are included in this section so they can be more easily identified and organized.

• **Tape measure**

This is very useful when taking long measurements: tailors use them when working with fabric. A ruler can be used instead for smaller pieces.

A) Iron; B) crimping pliers; C) round-nose pliers; D) cutting pliers; E) metal punch; F) wooden toothpicks; G) rubber stamps; H) metal cutters; I) pinking shears.

3 Processes

This chapter will introduce you to the processes through which wool is transformed into felt. You will see that different types of wool are obtained from different breeds of sheep. Some types of wool are easier to use than others for felting and this influences the ways it can be worked and its uses.

Likewise, wool is processed before it is used; after shearing, it must undergo several treatments that will then facilitate felting.

You will see that felting of wool can occur through both dry and wet processes with the use of different tools.

Wool

In this section you will see the process that wool undergoes from the moment it is shorn from the sheep until it is ready to be transformed into felt. Before working with it, it needs to be treated a little, cleaned, carded or combed, or even dyed. Depending on the breed of sheep, different results will be obtained; therefore the choice of wool will depend on the project you will be working on. To make an item of clothing, you can use smooth wool, such as that from Merino sheep. On the other hand, for pieces that will need to stand up to more regular use, wool from Tyrol sheep is more suitable.

Types of wool

Not all wools are equal; neither do they felt equally or have the same qualities in terms of how they feel; these differences depend on the breed of sheep. These factors play a significant role in the choice of wool for a particular piece, so try to select the wool best suited to the project at hand. The possibilities for the choice of wool may depend on the country where you live. If you are unsure of the characteristics of the wool found locally, you should do some tests to see how it felts before making any decisions. By doing this, you can avoid being disappointed and investing in pieces that turn out unsuccessful or do not produce the desired results.

Recently sheared, un-carded sheep's fleece.

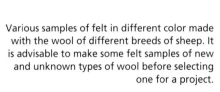

Various samples of felt in different color made with the wool of different breeds of sheep. It is advisable to make some felt samples of new and unknown types of wool before selecting one for a project.

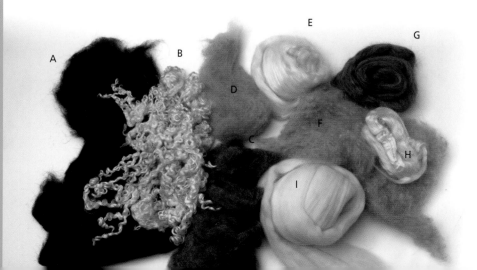

Selection of various natural, un-dyed wool: A) Karakul wool: from African sheep, has a rough texture and is a dark brown color, can be felted quickly and is ideal for carpets; B) Winsdale wool: does not felt well, but has an attractive crimp for decorations; C) Austrian Tyrol wool: a rustic-looking wool that felts well; D) Natural Karakul wool; E) Australian Merino wool: blended with silk, felts well, and the silk adds a very decorative luster; F) Spanish Merino wool: felts well, ideal for accessories, which come into contact with the skin due to its softness; G) Finnish wool: felts well and has a short, thick staple; H) Natural silk: does not felt but can be added to wool for decoration; I) Gotland wool: wool with a long staple that felts well.

Preparing the fleece

Once the fleece is shorn from the sheep, it still needs to be prepared before it can be felted, as it is still extremely dirty and full of dust, twigs, and rocks from the field. For this reason, the wool is laid out on the ground and the shepherd beats it with a stick to carry out the first cleaning, or skirting.

The process of preparing the fleece begins in this fashion and will eventually

Shepherd holding a sheep in preparation for shearing.

finish in a skein of wool. The process explained in this book is carried out by hand using traditional methods, but in reality, nowadays, this is done by machinery on an industrial scale to get the wool ready to be sold.

Shepherd beating the wool as part of the first skirting. By doing this, he removes the largest pieces of waste, which fall from the fleece easily.

Washing, dyeing, carding, and combing

After the first skirting, the fleece is then washed or scoured. The final step in the process is to eliminate the remainder of the urine, feces, blood, and sweat of the sheep from the fleece.

It is a slow process that requires drying the wool as well as washing it several times. Once completely dry, the wool can be dyed and carded.

The wool can be dyed at any point, but it is best to do so before carding it or after felting it, because if it is dyed after it has already been carded, it may felt too easily.

The process of carding the wool consists of passing the fibers between two cylinders with spikes, which eliminate residual vegetation caught in the wool; in addition, the spikes position the fibers in the same direction, making them run parallel to each other.

This is carried out today in an industrialized manner, but it is also possible to do it by hand, using hand carders or a drum carder. When using pre-dyed wool, you can also mix wool colors by carding.

The next step in preparing the wool involves passing the fibers through a series of very fine combs, allowing for the fibers to lie more uniformly in the same direction, thereby removing the shorter fibers.

Scouring the fleece to remove the traces of dirt still attached to it.

Dry wool, before it has been dyed.

Carding wool with a drum carder. In this case the wool has already been dyed and it is clear how colors can be mixed.

It is also possible to card the wool, as well as mix the colors, by hand using hand carders.

This preparation of the wool continues until eventually hanks of wool are formed which can be made into winter clothing. However for making felt, the wool first needs to be spun.

Carding the wool using a drum carder.

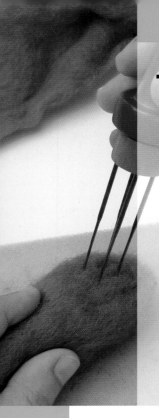

Turning wool into felt

If you look at wool fibers under a microscope, you are able to see how each fiber is formed from tiny scales. If these scales are subjected to stress, they open and begin to tangle with one another; the greater the stress the greater the tangle. This tangle, known as felting, is irreversible, as once the fibers are tangled together, they cannot be untangled. The stress in this process is caused by friction, which can be carried out with wet and dry processes, both of which will now be explained in detail.

Wet felting

The process of creating felt from wool using wet techniques consists in causing great stress in the woolen fibers and, at the same time, using hot water—at a recommended temperature of 104°F (40°C), or as hot as you can stand to put your hands in—and a mild soap without additives or colorants. You can use soap flakes dissolved in the hot water at a ratio of 0.05kg/l (about two tablespoons per liter of water) or use a bar of soap to lather up your hands or scrub the surface you wish to felt.

Either type of soap can be used, depending on which technique feels most comfortable. In some cases, you may want to cover your hands with plastic gloves, while in others, you may decide against it.

Using them facilitates the massaging process so the woolen fibers can become jumbled and stick together. However, there is no set rule; some artisans follow one method, while others opt for another. Ultimately, each individual must decide which method works best for him or her.

Phase 1: felting

The first step is to gently join the woolen fibers together. By lightly massaging the material, you will obtain a fabric that is quite uniform. For pieces that need to be hardwearing, you can also roll the material inside a bamboo mat to obtain a stronger felt.

However, the first stage of felting consists of massaging the material directly with your hands.

1- To create a flat fabric (in this case, a pistachio-green color), you will need a bamboo mat, a roller, a brush, a rubber band, a pair of plastic gloves, a nylon mesh cloth, plastic bubble wrap, a towel, and a hot bowl of soapy water (in this case with dissolved soap flakes).

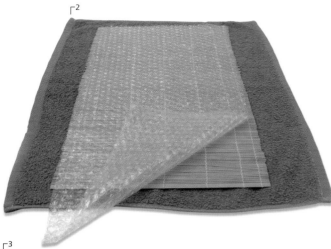

2- Lay out the towel so that it will soak up the water, place the bamboo mat on top, and then lay the plastic bubble wrap on top with the bubbles facing upwards.

3- Take pieces of the wool and place them vertically on the plastic to make the shape of a square.

4- Repeat the process, placing the wool horizontally until the square is complete. Depending on the project, it might be a good idea to measure or weigh the wool so that you have the same amount for each side of the piece.

5- Lay the nylon mesh cloth on top of the piece to prevent the pieces of wool from moving during the felting process. Using the brush, dampen it all over with the soapy water. You can use a sponge or your hands instead of the brush if you prefer.

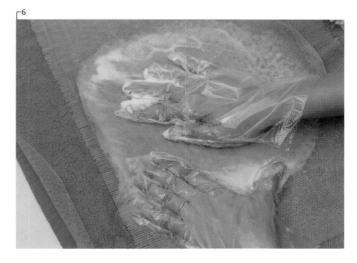

6- Put the gloves on and then lightly massage the entire surface with your hands, dampening it every now and then.

7- Carefully remove the nylon cloth, peeling off the woolen fibers which have stuck to it during the felting. Turn the woolen fabric over and massage the other side.

8- To make sure that the first layer of fabric has formed, do a simple test by pinching a piece of felt between your fingers to check that the fibers have bonded. If this is not the case, you need to massage the fabric a little more but if it is ready you can move on to the next stage of fulling the felt.

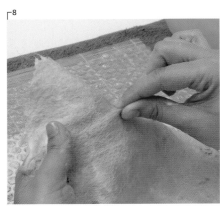

1- Place the fabric on top of the prepared work surface and then roll it up around the roller.

Phase 2: fulling

The felt is now subjected to a more forceful massage; however, not all felts should be fulled—the process should only be undertaken when you want to make the fabric very hardwearing. Bear in mind that during this phase, the wool may shrink to half of its initial size.

The process can be carried out in various ways, all of which work well. The choice depends on the characteristics of the project and the individual preference of the artisan working on the felt.

One of the methods used in these exercises is rolling the felt around a bamboo mat and roller, rolling it hard about 60 times on each side.

Another option is to hit the piece hard, several times, on the work table.

2- To stop it from coming undone, use the rubber bands to hold it in place. Roll it again sixty times and then repeat on the other side of the fabric. Now, remove the fabric and rinse it, hitting it across the table before rolling it up again in the bamboo mat. It is also a good idea to roll a little with the bubble wrap at the beginning and then continue on the piece without it when it has been rinsed, thereby giving it a rougher massage and enabling the wool to tangle more.

The correct way to roll is to position yourself so that your knees are slightly bent and the surface of the table is at waist height or a little higher so that you can roll the piece with your whole arm, from wrists to elbow.

3- Once you have finished, let the felt dry thoroughly and you will have a very strong fabric.

Dry felting

In order to turn wool into felt without using soap and water, you will need to use special felting needles. These needles must have a barbed end that is inserted into the wool in order to entangle the fibers, resulting in the creation of felt.

This process is slower than wet felting but it is more suitable for particular projects.

You can find various types of felting needles sold by different manufacturers; they are sold individually in different sizes that can be used together by fixing them onto a special handle, which can be used for large felting projects. You need a soft base to work on, made of foam rubber or EVA foam or even a brush with long bristles.

The following example of a simple pincushion will show you how this process works.

1- You will need a felting foam pad, four felting needles on a handle, a piece of green wool, a miniature flowerpot, and some pins.

2- Take the piece of green wool and wind it around itself in order to give it an elongated shape.

3- Place the piece on wool on the foam felting pad and jab it continuously with the felting needles until it felts.
Turn the wool around so that the needles can reach all parts of the piece.

4- Make grooves in the cactus with the individual felting needle by jabbing it up and down in lines until the whole of the cactus is completed.

5- Take another, smaller, piece of wool and felt it in the same way as the larger one. Next, join them together with the individual felting needle, fixing it as shown in the picture.

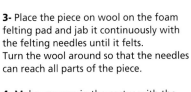

6- Once the felting is completed and the two parts of the cactus are joined together, add the pins and fix it inside the flowerpot. Add a little beach sand to enhance the colors.

c h a p t e r

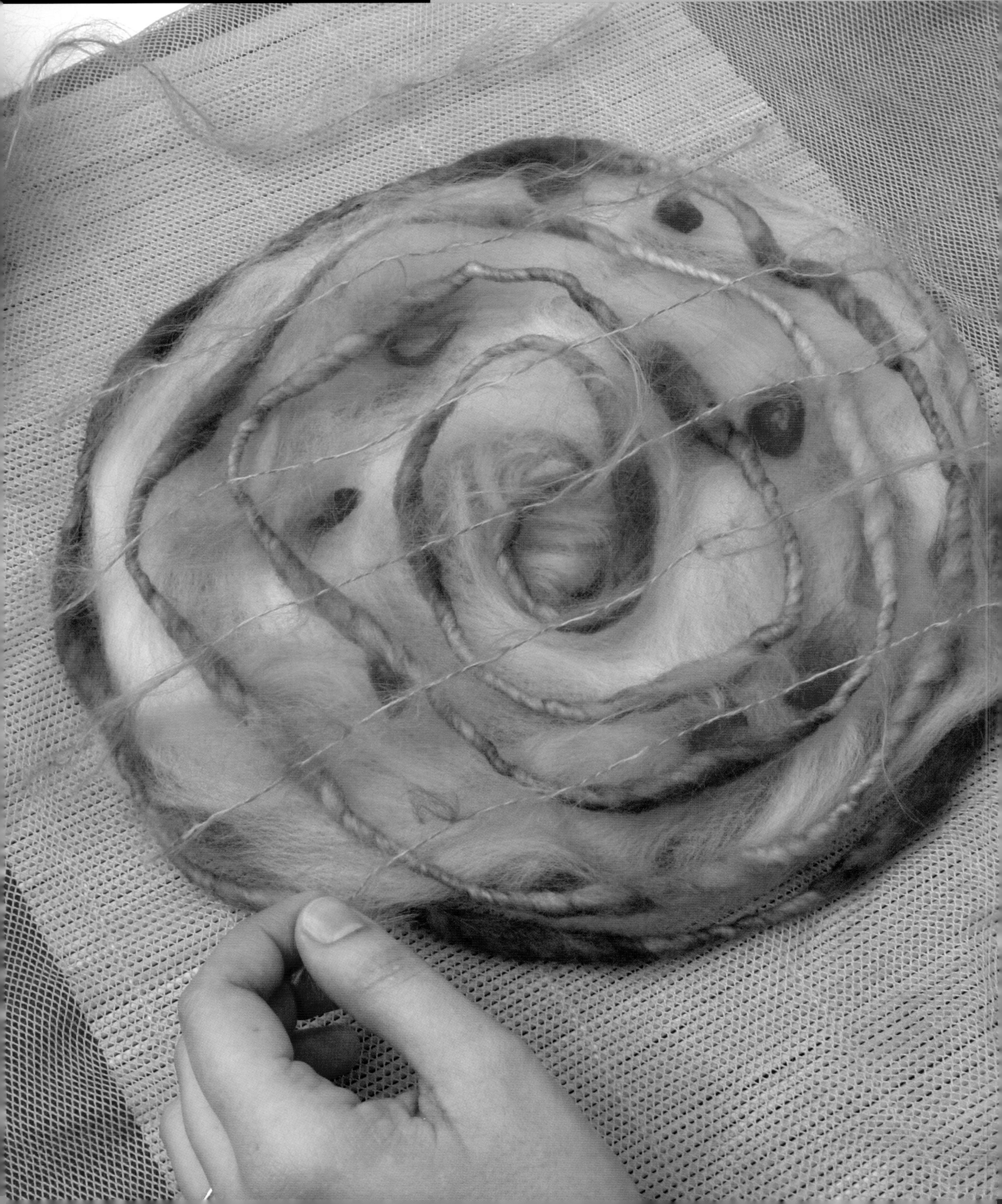

4 Techniques

This chapter explains various techniques
which have been collected, applied, and im-
proved by textile artists over the years.
Some of these ancient techniques are facilitated by the use of
everyday tools that make the work involved much less arduous.
You will see that there is no one set method of felting, and that often it is
possible to obtain similar results by using very different procedures. The
tools which are usually used for working with felt can be replaced if
need be: for example, using a roller in place of a broomstick or a
knitting needle.

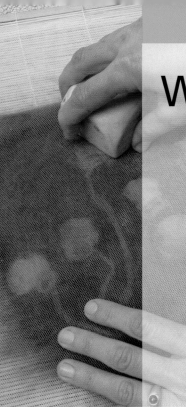

Working techniques

Next, you will see explanations of some of the different techniques that can be used in order to transform wool into felt. First, you will see how various decorations can be added to felt with both the wet and dry processes. You will also be shown how to make shapes from wool using the examples of three common shapes, how to use the nuno and cobweb techniques, how to give shape to the felt by using molds, and also how to felt in a washing machine.

Decorating wet felt

It is possible to add decorations to felt quite easily. You just need to take into account the type of material that you are going to add into the wool, as whatever you add will be "imprisoned" between the fibers during the felting process.

You can create fabrics using different colors and types of wool to obtain an attractive mix of textures and shades. It is also possible to add pieces of pre-felted cloth, woolen yarn, and other fabrics whose fibers are able to be worked into the felt.

You can give free reign to your imagination and create infinite possibilities; what's important is to experiment and explore with different fabrics and materials in order to achieve novel results.

You will now see you how to make a simple fabric, to which have been added some carded, colored wool, pieces of yarn from skeins of wool, and offcuts of pre-felted fabric. This will all be worked with the wet technique, using soap flakes dissolved in very hot water.

1- You will need carded wool in blue, white, and pink, plastic gloves, plastic bubble wrap, skeins of mohair wool in lilac and shades of orange, some star and heart shapes from offcuts of felt sheets, a towel, a nylon mesh cloth, a bamboo mat, a roller, several rubber bands, a brush, and a bowl of hot soapy water.

2- Lay out the towel and bamboo mat on the table and place the plastic bubble wrap on top of it. On top of these place the blue wool in two layers—one laid vertically and the other horizontally.

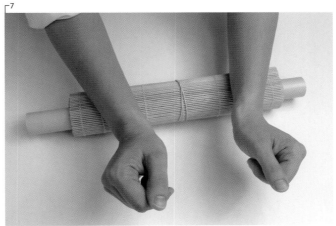

3- Next, position a small amount of pink wool, and on top of this a white star. Around this position a small amount of white wool in the shape of a circle.

4- To complete the design, add the rest of the decorations as you wish.

5- Cover the piece with the nylon mesh cloth, and use a brush to dampen it all over with hot soapy water. Put the gloves on and massage the fabric until the first layer of felt has been created.

6- Remove the nylon mesh cloth with care, and roll the whole piece around the roller.

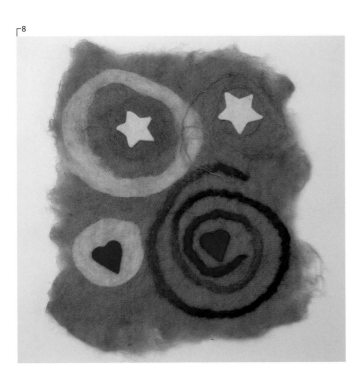

7- Place your arms in the position shown in the picture and roll across the fabric about 50 times on each side in order for the felt to be well fulled.

8- If necessary, repeat the previous step in order to achieve this. Then, rinse the fabric with cold water and leave to dry. All the decorations will have been fixed into place during the felting and fulling process.

Decorating dry felt

In order to create decorations on felt using dry techniques, the use of felting needles is essential—and you will need to have a number of these, as they break quite easily. The following example will show you how to decorate flat felt using craftwork cutters used for polymer clay, and also teach you how to decorate a felt shape (in this case, a ball of felt, from which you can create several objects once it is finished).

1- You will need the felting foam and felting needles, metal cutters, a ball of felt, red pre-felted fabric, and carded wool in white, blue, yellow, and bright pink.

2- Place the red fabric on top of the felting foam and then a metal cutter on top of this, then place a piece of white wool inside the hole of the cutter.

3- Jab the white wool continuously with the felting needle to felt it to the red fabric. Take care around the edges of the star so that they remain well defined.

4- Felt as many stars as you wish and finish them off by using the needle without the cutter.

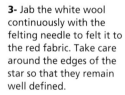

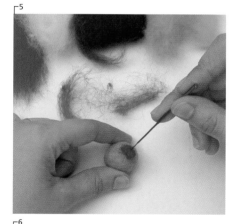

5- Now take the ball and pin to it and gently fix the piece of pink wool to it with the needle. The needle should go in and out vertically in order to prevent it from breaking.

6- With a little of the blue wool create an outline around the pink spot you have just made.

7- Add all the different colors of wool to complete the design. You can use this technique to decorate all kinds of felt objects, including some very detailed features.

Felt shapes

Another way of working with felt is making it into shapes.

In this section, you will see how to make a flower, a ball, and cord. These objects have been selected for their practical uses in other exercises. They are worked in different ways but all are made with soap and hot water, or in other words, with wet felting processes. They can also be created using dry-needle felting, but that process often takes much longer. For the flower and the cord, you will use a bamboo mat, and for the ball, you will just use your hands.

Felt flowers

Next, you will create a delicate but strong flower using two colors of Merino wool. With the help of a bamboo mat, soap and water, a plastic circular template, and a few other materials, you will see just how easy it is to create a strong matted fabric in the shape of a flower, which you can later use as an additional decoration or as a stand-alone piece.

1- You will need a towel, some scissors, a bamboo mat, a nylon mesh cloth, a tray, a sponge, a bar of soap, plastic bubble wrap, a plastic circular template, a rubber band, and a selection of orange and yellow wool.

2- Make a flat piece of two-colored felt by following the instructions described in the previous chapter, using hot soapy water and a sponge. Cut a circle with scissors, using the circular template.

3- Place the nylon mesh fabric, which you should have already dampened with soap and water, over the wool circle you have just cut out and massage it with your hands.

4- Using the scissors, cut out the shape of a flower from the circle.

5- Roll the piece up inside the bamboo mat and roll it between 60 and 70 times before removing it and rinsing it in order to eliminate the soap residue.

6- To finish, tie a rubber band around the end and allow it to dry.

7- Once dry, the felt will keep the shape of a beautiful flower.

Felt balls

Felt balls are very commonly used in felting projects and are often used as elements in necklaces and other types of costume jewelry, as they are both decorative and practical. In addition, once dry, this material is extremely lightweight, allowing it to be used in a great number of ways.

Next, you will see step by step instructions for a simple way to turn a ball of wool into felt using soap and water and the wet felting method.

1- You will need the following materials: a towel, blue wool, a bar of mild soap, and a bowl filled with hot water.

2- Put the wool into two or three layers, overlapping them vertically and horizontally.

3- Mold the wool with your hands until it forms a round shape.
Dampen it and then lather a little with the soap.

4- Next, making sure your hands are wet and soapy, roll the ball between them until it is tightly compressed and forms the right shape. This process should last between ten and fifteen minutes. Throughout the process, ensure that the water for wetting the ball is very hot and that you lather up your hands every now and then. To finish, press down hard on the ball as you roll it between your hands.

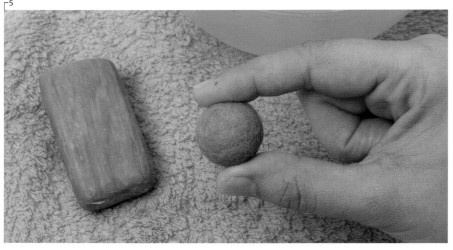

5- Once the felt ball is completely formed, rinse it well in cold water, adding a few drops of vinegar, if you wish, in order to set the colors.

Felt cords

Creating cords with wool is extremely entertaining, and the method is similar to that used for making sushi.

To prove this, see for yourself how easy it is to make a ring out of a knotted cord. To make the knots on this piece, you will need a ring sizer.

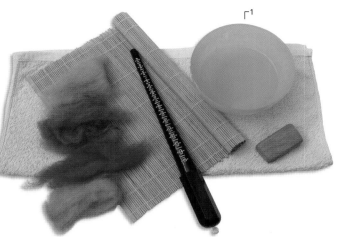

1- The materials you will need are a towel, a bowl of hot water, a bar of mild soap, a bamboo mat, blue, orange, beige, and green wool, and a ring sizer.

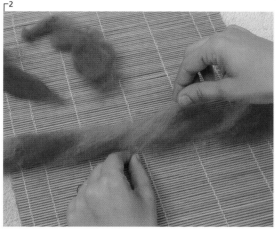

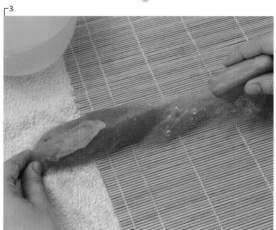

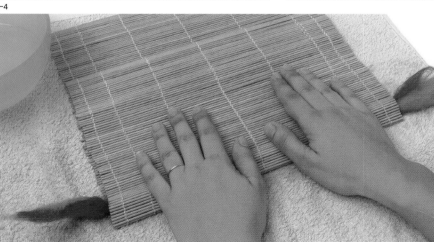

2- Lay out the towel and place the bamboo mat on top. Then, add the wool, dividing it into small pieces.

3- Wet the wool with soap and hot water.

4- Fold the bamboo mat over the wool and roll it hard several times until the wool forms a stiff cord. Fold the ends inside the mat so that they are also felted.

5- The cord is complete when it remains firm and stiff without losing its shape.

6- Put the cord under the ring sizer on the size you want the ring to be, and tie plain knots until you have made this fun ring.

Nuno felting

This is one of the most delicate techniques for working with wool; its name, *nuno*, comes from the Japanese word for cloth. The method consists of felting wool over a piece of fabric—usually silks, gauzes, and cotton—that has to be very lightweight and sheer rather than compact, otherwise the wool fibers cannot enter through the weft and allow felting to take place.

The process is slow, as wool must not felt too quickly; slow felting will allow the wool the amount of time needed to penetrate the fibers of the fabric. Once the felting has been completed, however, the results are usually remarkably beautiful, delicate, and very elegant, although, depending on the materials used, it is also possible to achieve very modern effects, which are much rougher and full of texture.

1- You will need warm, soapy water in a bowl, blue and pistachio-colored carded wool, plastic bubble wrap, a roller, a brush, a towel, rubber bands, plastic gloves, a nylon mesh cloth, and a piece of cotton mesh fabric.

2- Lay the towel out and place the plastic bubble wrap and cotton cloth on top. Add the wool in any pattern you like; here the threads of the blue wool have been teased and laid out flat.

3- Finish by placing all of the wool all around the cloth and then cover it with the nylon mesh cloth.

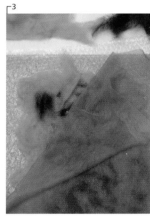

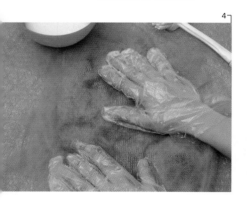

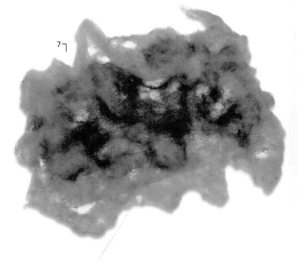

4- Using the brush, wet the area of the fabric with the design with soapy water and, wearing gloves, massage it with your hands. By doing this, the wool will be fixed in place and the colors and cotton cloth will not move around. Continue to massage patiently for a while; you can lift the nylon cloth every now and then and continue the massage without it.

5- Check that the first layer of fabric has become quite compacted and that it has joined to the cotton fabric. You can now begin the second part of the process: the fulling. Gently roll up the whole piece with a roller so that it does not crease.

6- Put some rubber bands around the roller to prevent the fabric from shifting inside it, and roll the piece around two hundred times before removing it. Turn the fabric over and continue to roll it another two hundred times.

7- Once it has all been felted together, and, depending on the type of fabric, you can continue to make very decorative textures. Rinse with cold water and leave to dry.

Cobweb felting

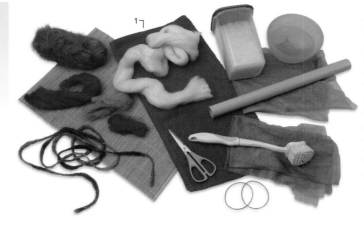

Together with *nuno* felting, this method is one of the most delicate techniques. It requires a great measure of patience, as the process is slow and tedious. The technique consists in felting by using only a very small amount of frayed wool. The hardest part of the process is rolling each side more than two hundred times.

The final result is a fabric that you can see through, and in some parts even put your fingers through. Pieces made in this technique are delicate and, as a result, are not suitable for frequent use. They are particularly appropriate, however, as curtains, table runners, and decorative placemats, but never for pieces requiring intensive felting, as the technique is called cobweb felting for good reason—precisely because the result has the appearance of a delicate, dust-coated spider web.

In the following exercise, you will see how to create a decorative placemat.

1- You will need white, pink, turquoise, and red wool, a skein of greenish color wool and some lilac-colored mohair wool, scissors, a roller, rubber bands, a bamboo mat, a towel, a bowl of water, soap flakes, and two nylon mesh cloths.

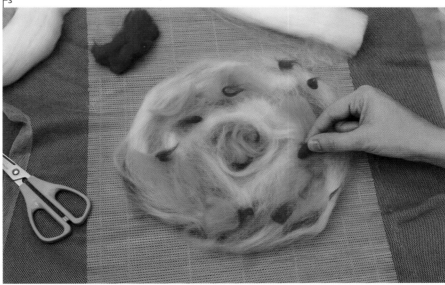

2- Lay out the towel and place the bamboo mat and one of the nylon cloths on top. Begin to add pieces of the wool to mark out your chosen design for the placemat.

3- You can cut out pieces of different colors of wool with the scissors and add them into the placemat little by little, taking care to keep the wool suitably frayed. Try not to compress the composition so that it remains light and airy.

4- Lastly, add some threads of lilac and green wool. Cover the materials with the other nylon cloth, taking care not to move the composition.

5- Using the brush, add some soapy water so that the following process will be easier.

6- Taking great care, roll up your complete composition in the bamboo mat.

7- Position the rubber bands around the mat to prevent it from shifting, then roll the composition around two hundred times before taking it out, turning it over and rolling it again another two hundred times before removing it from the mat.

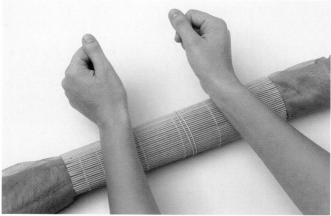

8- When finished, the resulting piece is very delicate. The design can be varied depending on the intended use of the piece.

Felting with molds

One very original and practical felting technique for creating shapes is by using containers and firm structures as molds. The basic procedure consists of lining the mold with wool and then massaging it with your hands, using water and a bar of soap for the felting. There are a number of ways of felting with wool and using a mold as a base: the example shown here uses a glass jar. Next you will see how to use a very common method to create a well-balanced, even piece.

You are going to create a container for storing pencils, paintbrushes, and the like.

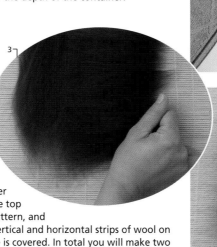

1- You will use one large towel and another smaller one, two bamboo mats, a container for water, a sponge, a bar of mild soap, a cylindrical container, plastic bubble wrap, some scissors, a tape measure, a felt-tip pen, a nylon mesh cloth, and Merino wool in dark green, light green, dark red, light red, bright pink, light pink, blue, turquoise, yellow, and orange.

2- With the tape measure, make a pattern from the plastic bubble wrap by measuring around a jar that is 9" round and 5" high. Divide the circumference in two; you are going to make two (flat) layers, but add approximately 30% more to compensate for future shrinkage in the fabric. Estimate with your eyes the depth of the container.

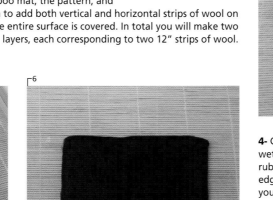

3- Cut the pattern and take four strips of green wool of 12" each in order to have the same amount of wool on both sides of the pattern. Place the small towel beneath the larger one to increase absorbency, and on the top of these place the bamboo mat, the pattern, and the nylon cloth. Begin to add both vertical and horizontal strips of wool on top of these until the entire surface is covered. In total you will make two layers, each corresponding to two 12" strips of wool.

4- Cover the layers with the nylon mesh cloth, wet the piece all over with the sponge, and rub it with the bar of soap. Next, leaving the edges dry, massage the rest of the piece with your hands.

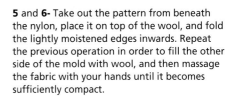

5 and **6-** Take out the pattern from beneath the nylon, place it on top of the wool, and fold the lightly moistened edges inwards. Repeat the previous operation in order to fill the other side of the mold with wool, and then massage the fabric with your hands until it becomes sufficiently compact.

7- Add another layer of green wool on each side, and then on top of these place the remaining pieces of colored wool for the decoration. Place the mesh cloth on top, dampen the fabric, and rub it with soap, then massage the piece before repeating the process on the other side. Remember to turn the edges inwards as you work.

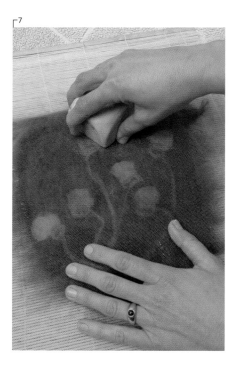

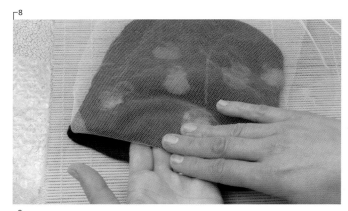

8- Once the wool has been felted, remove the mesh cloth and cut a strip across the top with scissors in order to remove the template from inside. With the help of the nylon cloth, massage the edges so they are even.

9- Now roll one bamboo mat inside the other to make a roller and roll it around fifty times before unrolling it. Repeat this step for each side of the piece.

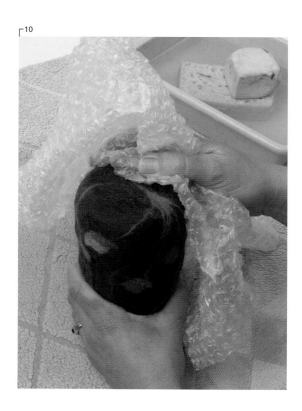

10- Place the felt around the jar that you are going to use as a mold. Wet it with soap and water and massage with the plastic bubble wrap to fit the felt to the shape of the container.

11- Rinse the piece to remove the soap residue and let it dry completely without removing the mold. It is now ready to be used as a pencil holder, for keeping paintbrushes, or as any other kind of similar container.

Felting in a washing machine

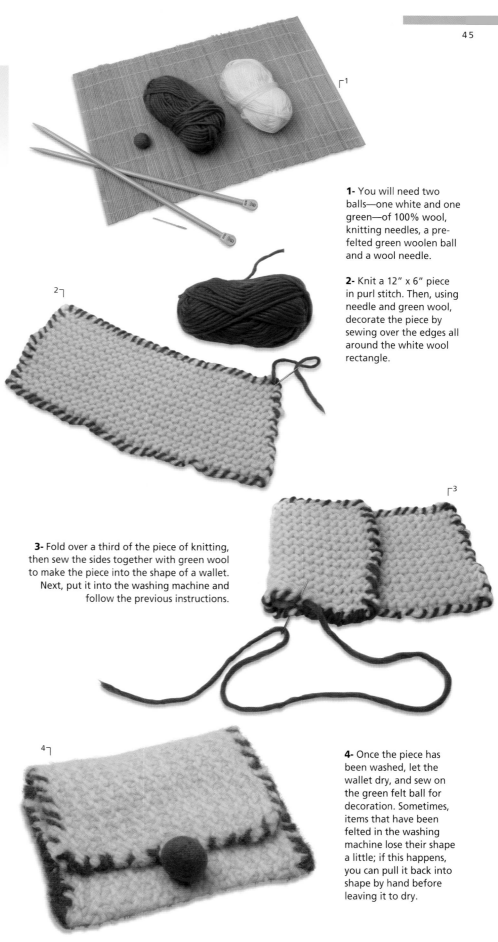

Another way of felting woolen pieces is by using a washing machine.

At some point or another, it is likely that everyone has accidentally shrunk a woolen garment in the washing machine and then tried unsuccessfully to stretch it back to its original shape. Unwittingly this woolen garment will have been submitted to the felting process and turned into felt.

Basically, the process of felting is submitting wool fibers to stress (see Chapter 3). One way to create stress is through friction, specifically by rubbing fabrics together with hot soapy water. This is exactly what a washing machine does: it rubs the garments together in the drum at high speed together with piping hot water and soap powder from the drawer. The item of clothing that is felted in the washing machine will not go back to its original shape and form because the process of felting is irreversible.

Nowadays, both ready-to-wear garments and knitting wool are given a protective treatment to make them machine-washable before they are sold, so the wool does not felt when it is washed.

For this project, once you have knitted the wallet, felt it in the washing machine by putting it in a special bag for delicate garments, and add various items of clothing you don't wear anymore for friction to aid the felting process. Put the soap in the soap powder drawer and wash the piece first on a short wash setting (about 20 minutes should be enough) and then change it to a temperature of about 104°F (40°C) with a spin cycle.

1- You will need two balls—one white and one green—of 100% wool, knitting needles, a pre-felted green woolen ball and a wool needle.

2- Knit a 12" x 6" piece in purl stitch. Then, using needle and green wool, decorate the piece by sewing over the edges all around the white wool rectangle.

3- Fold over a third of the piece of knitting, then sew the sides together with green wool to make the piece into the shape of a wallet. Next, put it into the washing machine and follow the previous instructions.

4- Once the piece has been washed, let the wallet dry, and sew on the green felt ball for decoration. Sometimes, items that have been felted in the washing machine lose their shape a little; if this happens, you can pull it back into shape by hand before leaving it to dry.

chapter

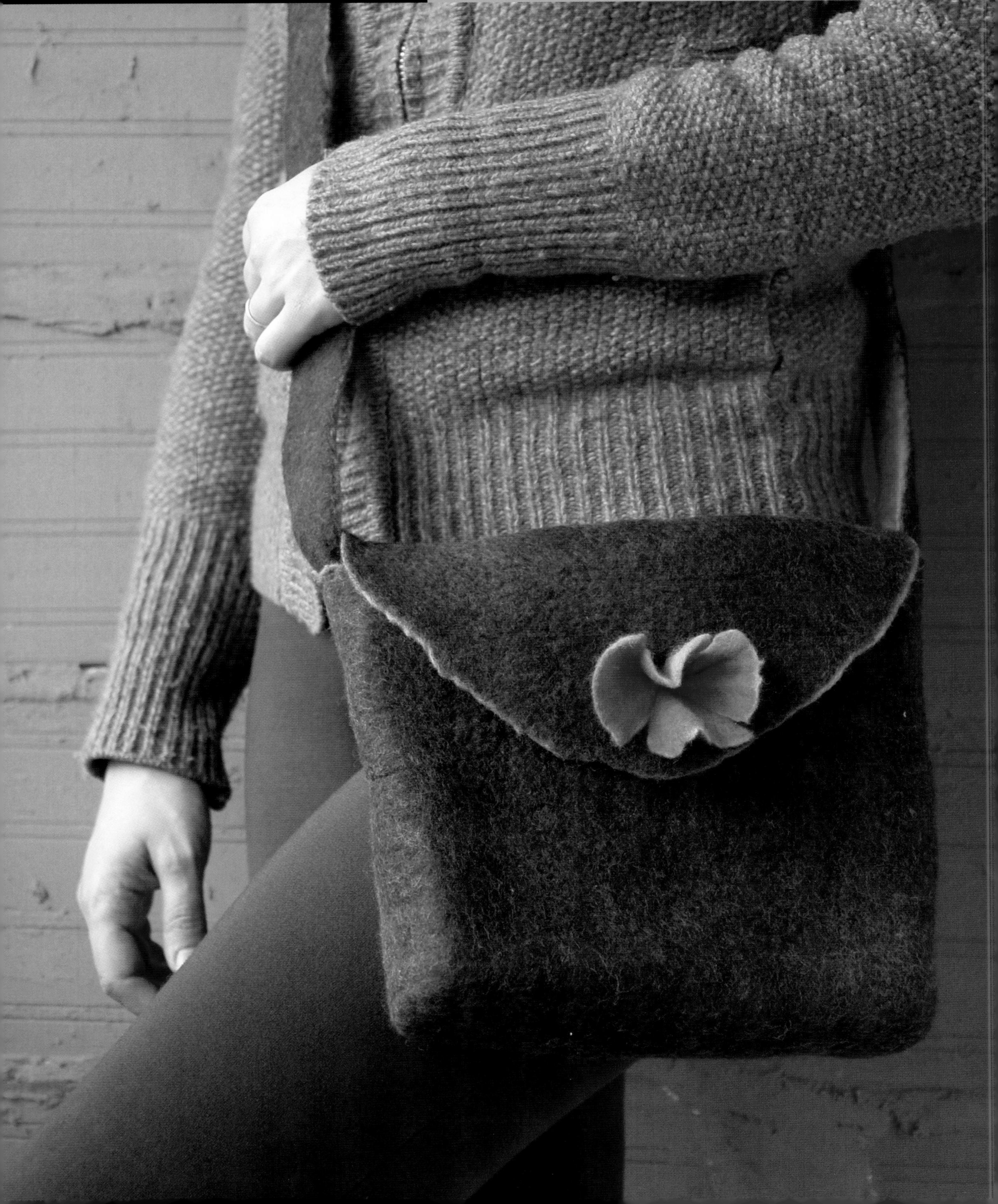

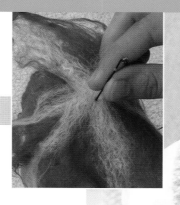

5

Projects

The following chapter describes various exercises step by step in great detail. These exercises, arranged from the easiest to the most complex, are divided into three sections.

The first section is dedicated to items for children and includes felting projects for decorating children's playrooms and bedrooms, as well dolls and other items for children. The second section will show you projects designed for making various articles and decorations for the home. Lastly, the third section gathers together some projects for making fashion accessories.

All of these projects allow you to start felting and gradually undertake more difficult projects as you become more experienced. You will work both with wool and commercially produced felt.

Felt for children

In this section dedicated to felt items for children, you will make some colorful projects using wet and dry felting techniques; in some exercises, you will only use commercially produced felt. These projects start off simply and increase in difficulty as you progress through them. The felting will be done with soap and water and also with needles. The projects enable you to make original puppets, hair scrunchies, brooches, decorated pencils, dolls, and interesting and unique wallets and coin purses.

Felt dreads scrunchie

You will now learn to create a fun scrunchie. By making this, you will learn to create felt cords using colored wool and the indispensable bamboo mat. This is a project that is very suitable for children as it is simple and you do not need any dangerous tools to make it. You will start by making a number of colored cords, from which you will make smaller cords that make the piece lighter.

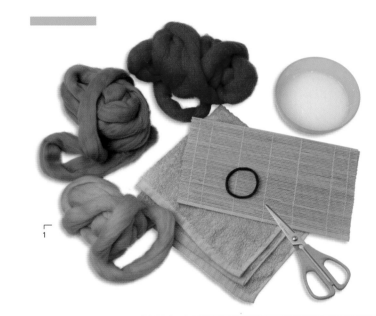

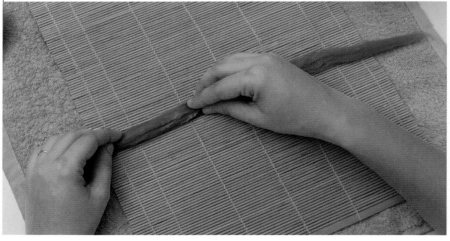

1- You need a bamboo mat, a hair elastic, a towel, a bowl with hot soapy water, some scissors, and mustard-colored, blue, and magenta Merino wool.

2- Lay out the towel and, on top of this, the bamboo mat. Next, lay a strand of wool on the mat like a cord and dampen it with your fingers.

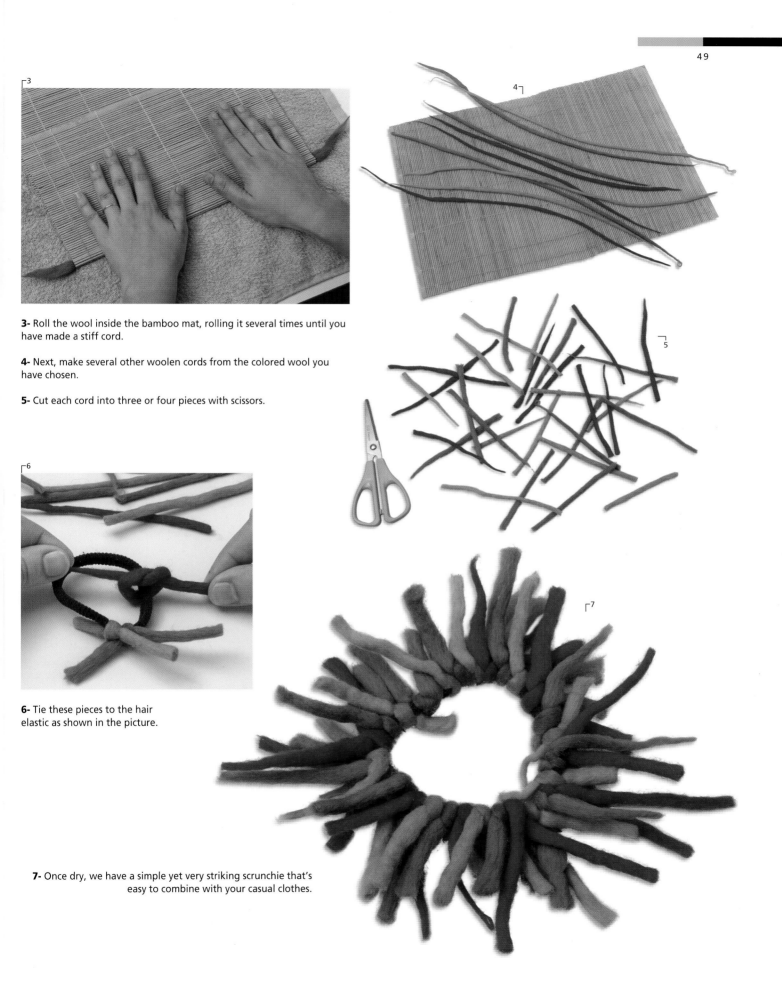

3- Roll the wool inside the bamboo mat, rolling it several times until you have made a stiff cord.

4- Next, make several other woolen cords from the colored wool you have chosen.

5- Cut each cord into three or four pieces with scissors.

6- Tie these pieces to the hair elastic as shown in the picture.

7- Once dry, we have a simple yet very striking scrunchie that's easy to combine with your casual clothes.

Bookmark

This project will show how to create a children's bookmark in the shape of a slice of watermelon. You will work with sheets of felt and will only need a few tools. This is a project which is very suitable for children as it is simple and you do not need any dangerous tools to make it.

This piece differs from the traditional bookmark shape of an elongated cardboard and paper rectangle. It takes the corner of a book as its starting point and uses a triangular shape that fits over the page rather than lying between the pages. By using this shape you can create an infinite variety of triangular bookmarks which fit over the upper corner of the page.

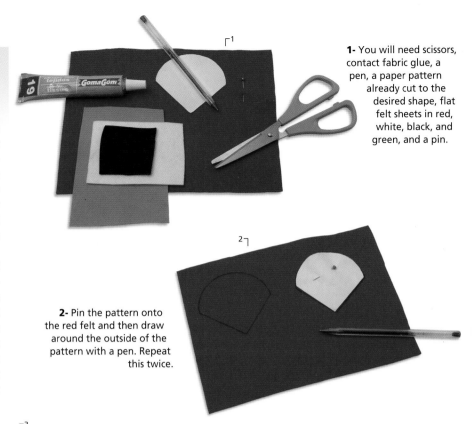

1- You will need scissors, contact fabric glue, a pen, a paper pattern already cut to the desired shape, flat felt sheets in red, white, black, and green, and a pin.

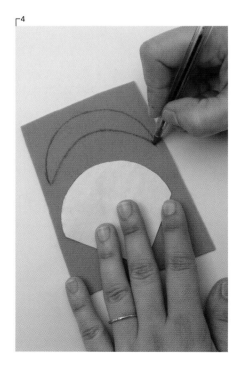

2- Pin the pattern onto the red felt and then draw around the outside of the pattern with a pen. Repeat this twice.

3- Cut out both parts of the pattern with scissors.

4- Using the paper pattern, draw what will be the rind of the watermelon. The upper part of this is done by following the upper part of the pattern, and the lower part is done freehand.

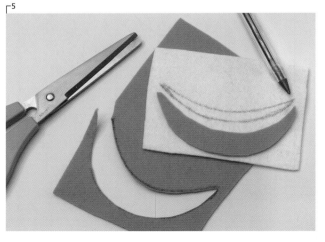

5- Use the same method to create the inside of the rind, which is white.

6- To make the characteristic watermelon seeds you do not need to make a pattern or draw them with pen, just cut them directly from the felt with scissors. For this piece there are seven seeds.

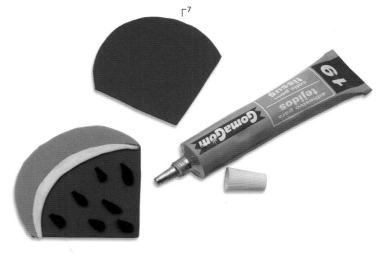

7- Use the fabric glue to stick the various parts of the watermelon slice together.

8- Spread the glue along the undecorated edge of the watermelon shape, stick both parts together, and leave to dry.

9- We have our fun and colorful bookmark ready to use.

Finger puppets

For this project, you will again work with flat, commercially produced felt. This is a very simple exercise which is great fun for young children to help with. You will learn how to make little finger puppets and if you wish, you can make funny characters for them and even decorate your hands to make a little puppet theater.

1- You will need scissors, fabric glue, a pen, peach, red, white, and black felt, a little combed black wool, and a paper pattern in the shape you have chosen for the puppets.

2- Draw around the pattern twice on the peach-colored felt and then cut them out.

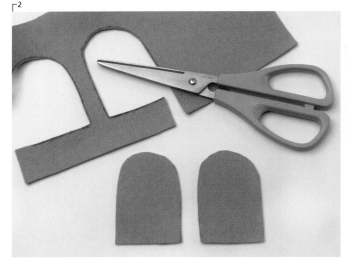

3- On the felt draw all the extra pieces for the puppets: hands, mouth, teeth, eyes, and nose. Draw them freehand, and then cut them out.

4- Glue all the parts of the face onto one of the main pieces of the puppet; you can change the expression of the puppet as you wish. Then glue the hands onto the other main piece of the puppet.

5- Glue the piece of black wool onto the piece with the hands. Tease it out to make hair for the puppet.

6- Apply glue to the edges of one of the pieces, leaving the bottom edge unglued. Stick the two main pieces together.

7- Your final result: fun finger puppets to entertain the children.

Postcard

You can make fun postcards with your children to send to friends and relatives, designed for specific occasions and with the recipient's individual tastes in mind.

Next you will make a colorful retro postcard reminiscent of the 1960s. This exercise only uses commercially produced felt and no dangerous tools are used, so it is an ideal project for children to help with.

1- For this exercise you will need scissors, fabric glue, a piece of white cardboard approximately 4" x 6", green, black, purple, red, yellow, white, blue, and brown felt, white fabric paint, and a rubber stamp.

2- Use the piece of cardboard as a base and cut the green felt to the same size, Apply glue to the edges of the felt to join them together.

3- Draw all the pieces of your chosen pattern onto the colored felt.

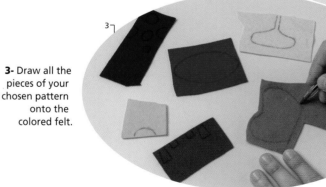

4- Once all the pieces have been drawn, cut them out, ensuring that the pen marks cannot be seen.

5- Glue on the pieces with a little fabric glue and leave to dry.

6 and **7-** Cut a square of black felt. Put a little white paint on some aluminum foil and then place the stamp in the paint, making sure the surface is covered. Now print onto the felt.

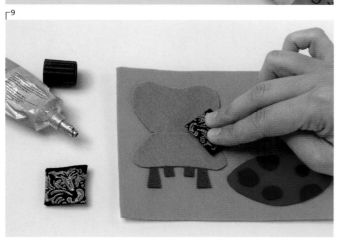

8- Once dry, cut the stamped felt into two rectangles and fold them over some small pieces of felt so that they look like two stuffed pillows.

9- Glue the pillows onto the chair on the postcard.

10- You can choose an envelope in the same color as the chair to bring out the colors of the piece.

Christmas fridge magnet

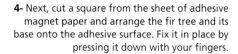

The following project also uses only commercially produced felt. Here it is used to make Christmas themed fridge magnets that you can change as you wish or you can use the technique to create other designs.

It is a simple project and can be done with children, as it does not involve any tools that are dangerous to them.

1- You will need pieces of felt of various colors: pistachio green, dark green, light and dark brown, yellow, red, white, orange, and turquoise, scissors, fabric glue, a pen, and a sheet of adhesive magnet paper.

2- Draw a fir tree shape on the pistachio-colored felt. Now draw what will be the shadow on the dark green and also the colored baubles.

3- Cut the designs out. Also cut out the tree trunk in light brown and its shadow in dark brown.

4- Next, cut a square from the sheet of adhesive magnet paper and arrange the fir tree and its base onto the adhesive surface. Fix it in place by pressing it down with your fingers.

5- Trim away the leftover adhesive magnet paper so that you are left with the shape of the fir tree.

6

6- Apply glue to each of the layers of the tree with a toothpick and stick them one on top of one another until you have achieved the final design.

7

7- You can create variations on the fir trees and make them into a Christmas forest to decorate and personalize your refrigerator and your kitchen.

Candy brooch

This project demonstrates that a great deal of effort is not necessary in order to achieve original results. You can use felt to create fun imitations of real things by looking around at everyday objects to find endless sources of inspiration. The example shown here uses some mouth-watering sweets to make a brooch that is both "sweet" and fun.

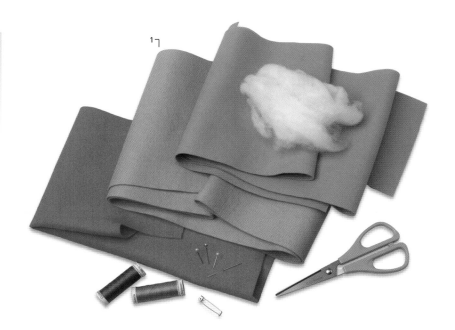

1- The materials needed for this exercise are scissors, some orange and green threads, a brooch back, needle and pins, stuffing and pink, peach, and pistachio-colored felt.

2- Cut a square of each color felt.

3- Make small cuts lengthways at both ends of each square.

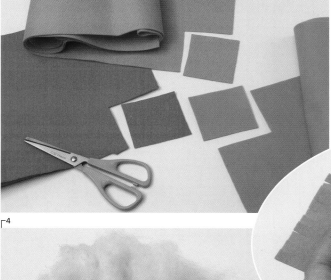

4- Place a ball of stuffing in the center of each piece of cut felt.

5- Roll up the felt square and secure with a pin to prevent the ends from coming undone.

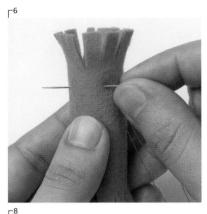

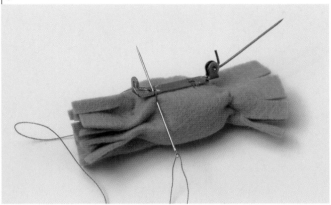

6- Thread the needle with green thread and stitch around each end.

7- Pull the thread so it gathers the ends to look like a candy wrapper. Repeat this process for the other end of the piece of candy.

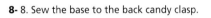

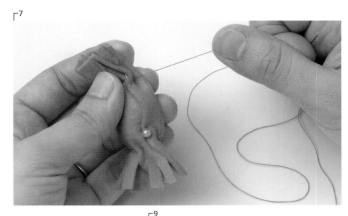

8- 8. Sew the base to the back candy clasp.

9- Repeat the process for the felt squares in pink and peach and then join each of them together by sewing them at one end.

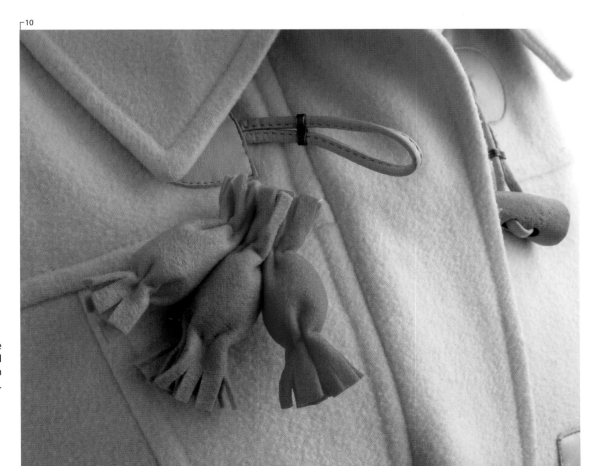

10- Now you have a simple and novel brooch to adorn any lapel.

Piglet Pen

The next project is a cute little pig with a pen inside it. For this you will work with carded wool, which is more comfortable to felt, and use a mix of techniques. For the base of the pig you will need soap and water while needle felting will be used for the join. You will also learn how to use needle felting and small pieces of wool to create expression and shapes.

1- You will need a towel, a bar of soap, a bowl for hot water, a bamboo mat, felting foam, pink, burgundy, and black carded wool, a large felting needle, and a pen.

2- Moisten a little of the pink wool in hot soapy water and make a compact ball for the head of the piglet.

3- Rest the head on the felting foam, take a tiny ball of burgundy felt and place it on the head. Next, use the felting needles to jab the two balls a number of times until they are joined together. Begin with the edges, jabbing diagonally, and then cover the whole of the surface to make the shape of a snout.

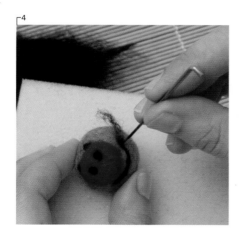

4- Use the needle to jab in little pieces of black wool to make the eyes, the nostrils, and the mouth of the piglet.

5- Next wet the pink wool with soapy water and create two tiny little balls, pressing them a little to flatten them. With the needle, add a little burgundy-colored wool to the inner part of the shape to make the piglet's ears.

6- Place a little pink wool around the ears to attach them to the head with the needle.

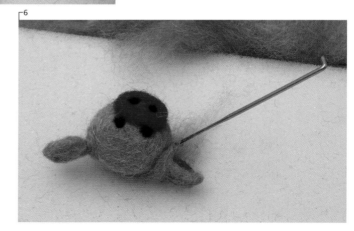

7- Next, wrap the pen in pink wool by placing it in the center of the wool, dampening it with soap and water and rolling the wool up around it.

8- Roll the whole thing up in the bamboo mat and roll it between sixty and seventy times before removing it from the mat.

9- After checking that the felt has compacted and joined to the pen properly, add the head. For this add pink wool between the pen and the head and use the felting needle until the sides are well joined. You will need to jab repeatedly and patiently as it will take a while for the piece to become stiff and even.

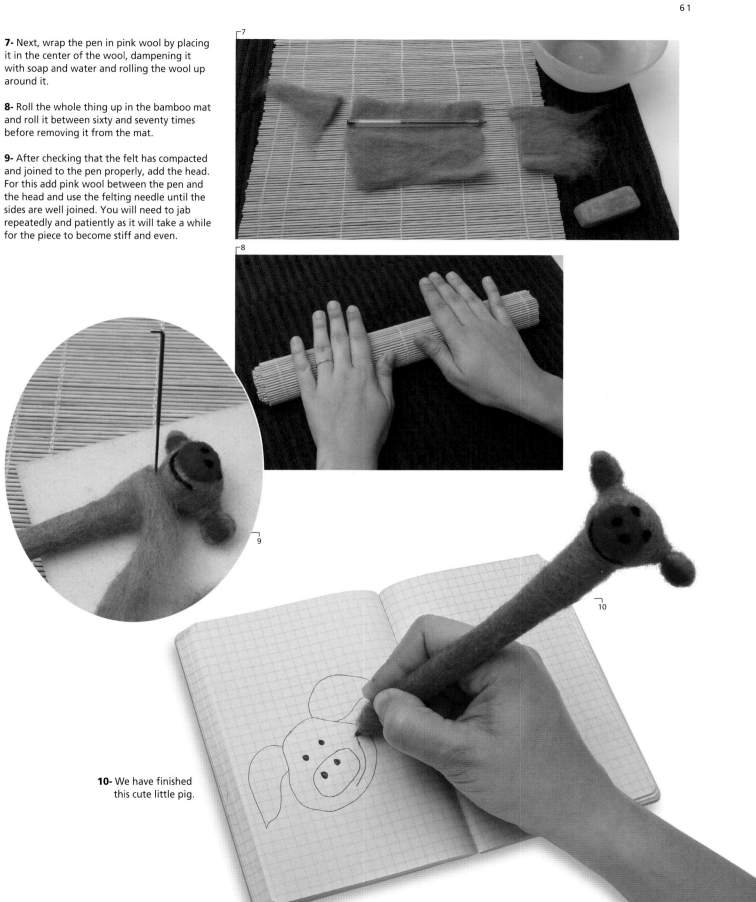

10- We have finished this cute little pig.

Woolen doll

Next, you will see how to make a cute felt doll just by using needle felting. You will need three different gauges of needle, each with a specific job to do. You will also use different wools, which, depending on where they come from and the combing and carding process, will take a different amount of time to felt. The piece uses different colored Merino, some wool that takes longer to felt because it is combed until only the long fibers are left, and also carded Tyrol wool, which felts quickly as it has both long and short fibers.

1- You will need a wooden toothpick with a pointed end, a felt-tipped marker, a ruler, a foam felting pad, large felting needles, medium felting needles, small felting needles, some 0.5-inch-thick EVA foam, turquoise and mustard-colored Merino wool, navy blue, pistachio, flesh-colored, bright pink, heather, and red carded Tyrol wool, and a carded white Tyrol wool, which is much coarser and therefore cheaper and will be used to stuff the doll.

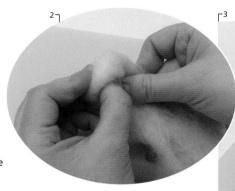

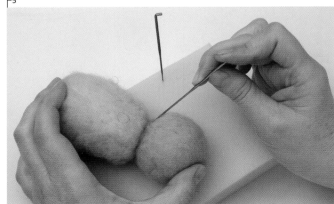

2- Take an elongated piece of white wool and roll it around itself to make a ball of about 1.5" for the head of the doll.

3- Rest this on the foam felting pad and use the medium needle to jab the entire ball until it becomes compact and well-felted.

4- Next, cover the white ball with flesh-colored wool, using the fine felting needle so as not to leave behind marks or holes.

5- In order to create the body, repeat the process at the beginning of the exercise. Roll up a piece of white wool around itself until it is the desired shape, in this case around 2.5" high, and felt with the medium needle. Then, join the head and body by placing one piece on top of the other and use both the medium and small needles to felt them together, as shown in the picture.

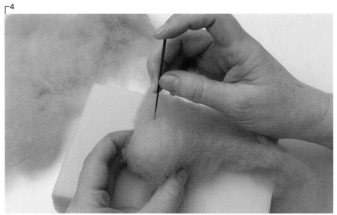

6- To make the neck, take another strip of flesh-colored wool, wrap it around where the neck should be and fix it with the medium needle.

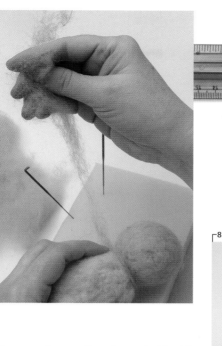

7 and **8-** Next make the arms by measuring out 4" on the toothpick with the ruler and felt-tip marker. Then, roll white wool around the marked section of the toothpick.

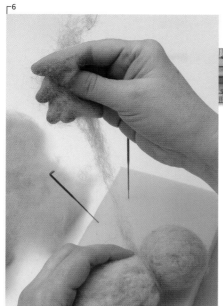

9 and **10-** Now make a hand by wrapping flesh-colored wool around the end of the toothpick. Cover the rest with navy blue wool to create a sleeve.

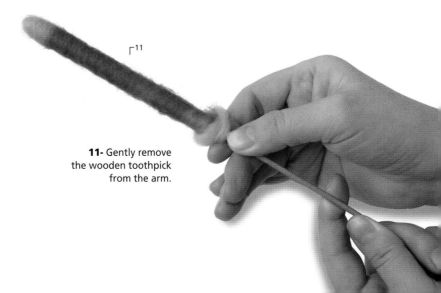

11- Gently remove the wooden toothpick from the arm.

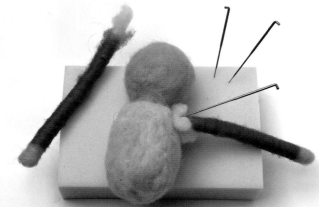

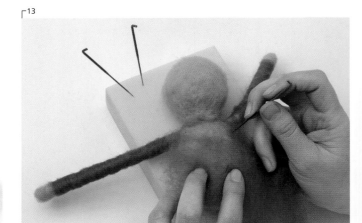

12- Repeat the process to make the other arm and then attach both arms to the body with the medium needle.

13- Cover the body with navy blue wool using the medium felting needle.

14- Add the details of the face with the small needle.

15- Attach the mustard-colored wool onto the head to make the hair, and for decoration, make the hair into two topknots and wrap a little red wool around them.

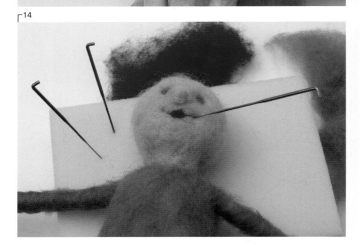

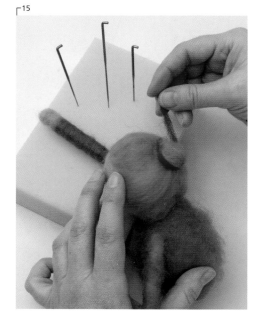

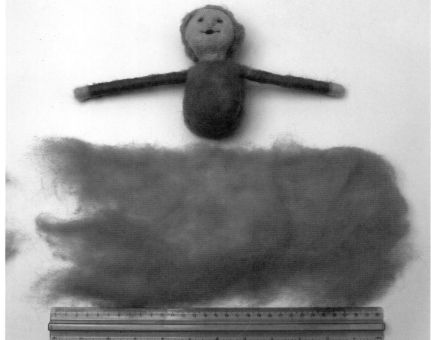

16- For the skirt, prepare a piece of green wool about 12.5" long and 12.5" wide, more or less double the size of the body, so the skirt covers it completely.

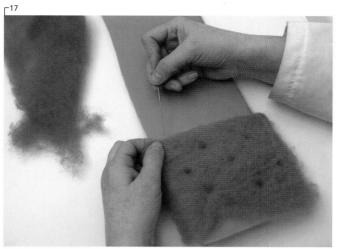

17- Using the felting foam as a base, felt and decorate what will be the skirt of the doll with the large needle. Jab the felt to make the edges of the skirt.

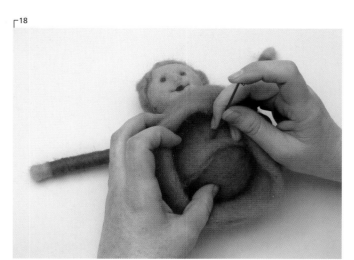

18- Join the skirt to the body of the doll.

19- Make the two legs in the same way you made the arms. However, this time, use a piece of blue wool to make striped stockings. Join the legs to the body using the large felting needle.

20- Once the arms and legs have been joined to be body you will be left with a charming ballerina-type doll, ideal for decorating children's bedrooms.

Children's coin purse

This project is a pretty little children's coin purse with a strap in pastel colored wool. For this piece you will use the technique of felting with molds: in this case a circular mold of stiff cork will be used as the inner template when felting the wool. You will also see how to add a handle which, as it is felted at the same time as the base, becomes part of the same fabric.

1- You will need a towel, plastic bubble-wrap, nylon mesh cloth, a bamboo mat, a sponge, a bowl with hot soapy water, a pair of scissors, fabric glue, needle and thread, mustard and lilac colored wool, a circular cork mat, a stick to use as a roller, and several small pre-felted colored balls.

2- Lay the bamboo mat on top of the towel to make a cord from the lilac wool by following the process explained in Chapter 3. Leave the ends unfelted.

3- Next, put some pieces of frayed mustard-colored wool on top of the circular cork mat. Make two layers of threads, one horizontal and the other vertical.

4- Cover the whole thing with the nylon mesh cloth and use the sponge to wet it with the soapy water. Then massage it with your hands until you obtain a fabric that is quite even.

5- Remove the nylon fabric and repeat the process on the other side, but this time putting down only a fine layer of mustard wool. Once you have obtained a fabric that is quite compact, add the cord that you made at the beginning of the exercise and on top of this put down the rest of the second layer of mustard-colored wool.

6- Cover the piece with the nylon fabric, wet it with the sponge soaked in soapy water, and massage it with your hands.

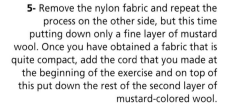

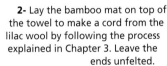

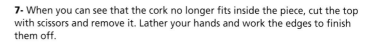

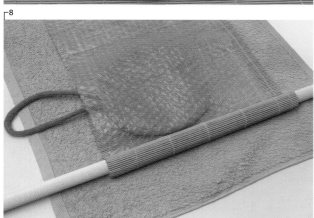

7- When you can see that the cork no longer fits inside the piece, cut the top with scissors and remove it. Lather your hands and work the edges to finish them off.

8- Lay the purse onto the bamboo mat and the towel and cover it with the plastic bubble wrap. Use a stick to roll the project up together and begin the second part of the felting process—the fulling—which involves rolling it around fifty times before removing it.
Repeat this procedure on each side of the coin purse.

9- Once the coin purse is dry, add on the little felt balls. You can glue or sew them on; the two balls which will be the buttons should be sewn on to make them more secure, but the others are just for decoration.

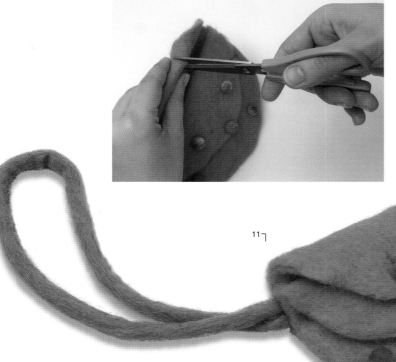

10- Use scissors to cut slits in the purse; these will act as buttonholes for the little balls to go through and keep the purse more securely shut.

11- The result is a delicate coin purse with a handle that allows it to be held easily.

Variations

In this final section, you will see various examples of pieces made with felt; they are made with the same techniques in this chapter dedicated to felt craft for children. In the following examples you will find sources of inspiration that will allow you to be even more creative in your projects. These pieces have been created by different artists around the world and combine both wet and dry felting techniques, using handmade and commercially produced felt. You will see dolls, magnets, postcards, covered pens, finger puppets, coin purses, and more.

Best friends, made from felt. Natalie Kalinova, Australia.

Small felt coin purse with handle, felted with soap and water. Elvira López Del Prado, Spain.

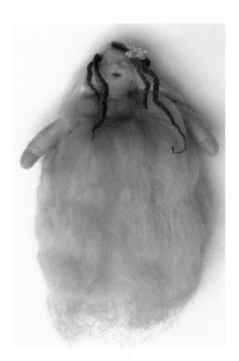

Nymph felted with needles. Mercé Puig, Spain.

Magnet made using commercially produced felt. Elvira López Del Prado, Spain.

Wool covered pen, felted with soap and water. Elvira López Del Prado, Spain.

Various pencils made from commercially produced felt. Isabel Martínez Narro, Spain.

Children's coin purse made from colored felt. Dolores García Miguel, Spain.

Postcards made from commercially produced felt. Elvira López Del Prado, Spain.

Felt bookmark. Elvira López Del Prado, Spain.

Finger puppets made from commercially produced felt. Goiuri Ochoa Munárriz, Spain.

Felt and the home

The inside of a house reflects the personality of the people who live in it. In order to help to combine the different elements that embellish a home, this chapter will show you a series of colorful exercises, each more difficult than the one before.

Among the proposed projects are pillows, lamps, coasters, felt tapestries, bugs to decorate flower pots, table runners, mirrors, decorative mobiles, and bowls. In all these projects, you will apply the techniques you have learned in this book, working with commercially produced felt as well as felting wool.

Abstract design pillow

As you complete projects, you will end up with many left over pieces and offcuts of materials. You can keep these to use in future projects such as the following exercise.

You can make and personalize pillows by using offcuts of colored felt to decorate them. Here, the combination of bright cheerful colors opens up many possibilities.

For this project you will use a sewing machine to stitch the pillow as this makes it much easier to complete and is faster than sewing by hand. However, the project can be done perfectly well by hand using needle, thread, and a little patience.

1- You will need blue felt, scissors for cutting paper, tailor's chalk to mark the fabric, pins, stuffing, pinking shears, sewing thread, and cardboard cut to the size of the pillow. You will also use a sewing machine for stitching (you can sew by hand if you prefer).

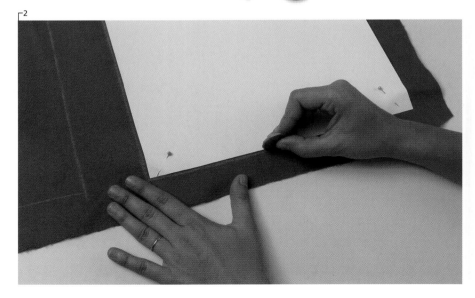

2- Pin the cardboard onto the felt and draw around the outside with tailor's chalk. Repeat this process twice, for both sides of the pillow.

3- Cut out the two pieces of the pillow, leaving a little extra all around, as shown in the picture.

4- Lay out the felt to get an idea of what the final design for the pillow will look like.

5- Begin to sew, in this case, with the machine.

6- Sew the offcuts onto the pillow one at a time so that it is easier to see the composition of the design.

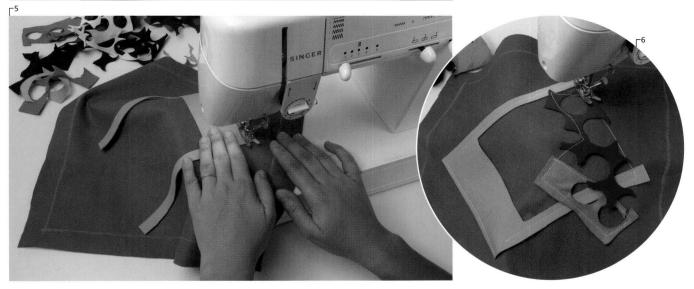

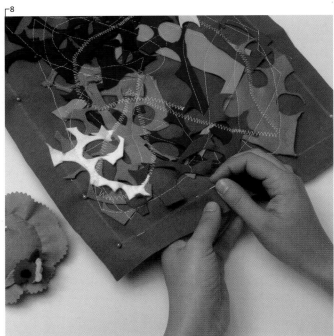

7- The final design will look like this.

8- Pin the two sides of the pillow together, following the chalk lines.

9- With the sewing machine join three of the four sides of the pillow, using the pins as a guide. Leave one side open.

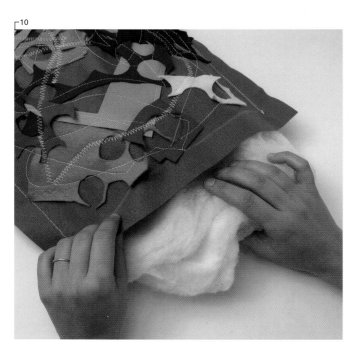

10- Fill the pillow by adding stuffing through the open side until it is the right shape.

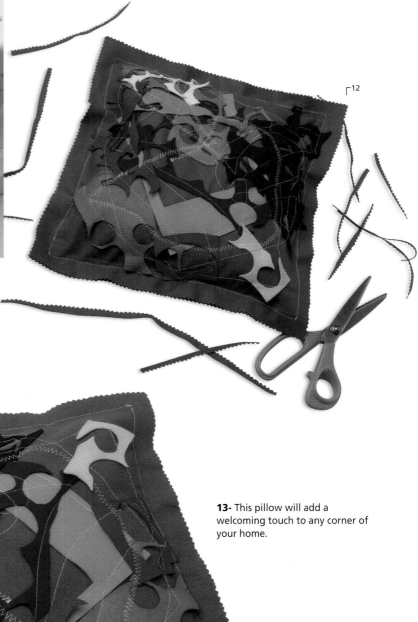

11- Use the sewing machine to sew up the final side.

12- Lastly, use the pinking shears to trim the edges of the pillow and finish off the decoration.

13- This pillow will add a welcoming touch to any corner of your home.

Baroque lamp

This lamp will create a warm atmosphere in a room by adding a touch of red. To do this you will make an ornate Baroque-style lamp with commercially produced felt.

Using this design as a base, it will be easy to change the style of the lamp just by changing the color of the felt and making various cuts with scissors. This exercise is simple to do and once it is finished you can add a modern lamp base and show it off in your home.

1- You will need red felt, a lamp base, scissors, fabric glue, tailor's chalk, pins, and a ruler.

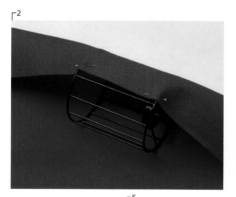

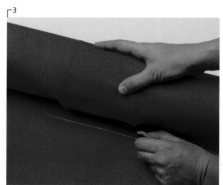

2- Cut the felt to the width of the lamp. Next, attach it, using pins, to the base of the lamp to keep the cloth taut.

3 and **4-** Turn the lamp around, keeping the fabric taut, and mark the edge with chalk either with a ruler or free hand. Cut the edge with scissors.

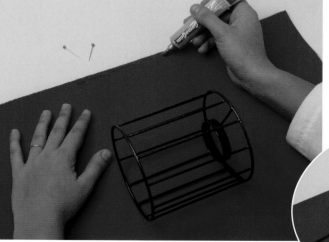

5- Put glue along the edge of the fabric.

6- Hold the fabric in place using pins to prevent the two ends you are gluing from coming loose.

7- Cut strips all around the lamp at both the top and bottom ends, taking care to cut the strips of varying thicknesses to make the design more dynamic. Do not cut further than the edge of the lamp, otherwise the metal rim of the lamp will show and the piece will not be so attractive.

8- Taking each piece one at a time, apply glue to the inside of the end of each one.

9- Use pins to hold everything in place while the glue dries.

10- Once you have chosen the lamp base to go with the lampshade, put the piece in a place where it creates the best effect.

Coasters

This project will show you how you can take advantage of all the off-cuts and scraps of felt left over from previous projects.

You will create a fun coaster made from offcuts of commercially produced felt sewn together. These coasters are both washable and reversible.

For this piece, a sewing machine is essential, simply because there are so many stitches involved.

This piece is novel because of the material it uses: water-soluble Vilene, a type of interfacing that dissolves in cold water and is used in the making of individual felt, cloth, and woolen pieces that would be impossible to make without it.

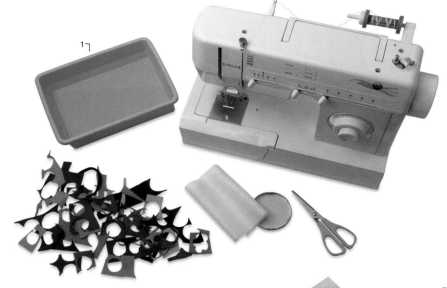

1- For this exercise you will need offcuts of commercially produced felt left over from previous projects, a container of cold water, a rectangular piece of water-soluble Vilene, scissors, a pen, a circular object to use as a template (here, the lid of a container), sewing thread and, a sewing machine.

2- Use a pen to draw around the lid onto the water-soluble Vilene. Later, these marks will serve as a guide for sewing.

3- Assemble your design onto one of the bases you have drawn, choosing contrasting colors. Layer the offcuts until there are no gaps not covered in felt.

4- For decoration, cut some even smaller pieces from the offcuts.

5- Fold the Vilene in half and match it up to the circle marked with your design.

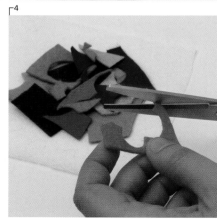
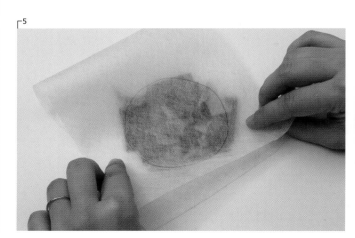

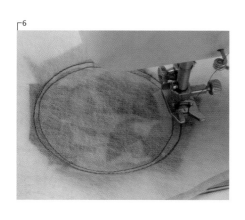

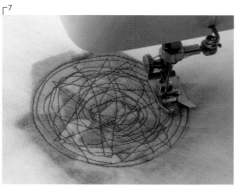

6- Using the sewing machine, stitch along the lines you have drawn in pen; sew a couple of circles to start off.

7- After, sew randomly over the surface of the design without going outside of the initial outline.

8- Trim away the remaining Vilene with scissors.

9- Submerge the coaster in cold water for a few seconds, gently rubbing it between your fingers to help the Vilene dissolve.

10- Using this technique, you can make as many coasters as you wish to decorate your home.

Tapestry

It is possible to work with wool as if it were paint, creating delicate works to cover the walls of your favorite rooms.

In the following exercise, you will see how to make a small felt tapestry of small dimensions. However, if you wish, you can increase the amount of materials and use this technique for a larger project.

The tapestry shown here uses vibrant shades over a soft, off-white background, but you can use your creativity freely with this decorative technique once you have learnt how to make designs by placing layers of wool on top of the other before felting them.

1- You will need white and mustard-colored Merino wool, a ball of white wool, a ball of charcoal gray bouclé wool, mild soap flakes, natural and without additives, which will be dissolved in a bowl of water, a brush, a towel, rubber bands, a bamboo mat, two plastic bags, a nylon mesh cloth, and plastic bubble wrap.

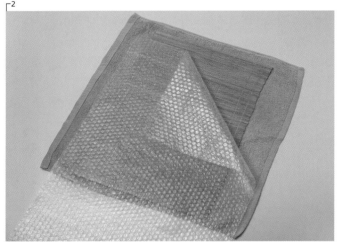

2- First lay out the towel, then put the bamboo mat on top and lastly place the plastic bubble wrap with the bubbles facing upwards.

3- You are going to make a felt tapestry with a drawing of a plant with small flowers. First, using the gray bouclé yarn, lay out the design of the branches. If you prefer, you can place a pre-drawn design under the bubble wrap to serve as a guide.

4- Next, place some small pieces of mustard-colored wool, which will be the flowers.

5- Add the white wool, taking into account the direction of the fibers and placing them alternately horizontally and then vertically to facilitate the felting process. Put down three layers of white wool to strengthen the tapestry.

6- Dissolve the soap in hot water (see Chapter 3 for the suggested ratio), and add the solution little by little to the wool, distributing it well with a brush.

7- Cover the piece with the mesh cloth. Put plastic bags over your hands and secure with rubber bands. Flatten the felt tapestry by pressing down all over the surface of the piece in order to eliminate all the air from inside the woolen fibers.

8- Rub in a circular motion while continuing to press down all over the surface. Every now and then, add some more soapy water. This process will take a while for the first felting to take place.

9- Remove the mesh cloth carefully, as many of the wool fibers will have stuck to it, and you will need to disentangle them.

10- Turn the project over and repeat the previous step.

11- When you think that a fabric has formed, you can carry out a simple test to check. To do this, hold the fibers of the cloth between your fingers and try to separate them. If you cannot do so, this means the wool has become a fabric that is ready for the next step of fulling the felt. However, if the fibers separate easily, you will need to repeat your previous steps, using the plastic bags on your hands and soapy water for a few minutes longer.

12- The next step is to rinse the felt tapestry in very cold water, removing the excess moisture with a towel or absorbent paper.

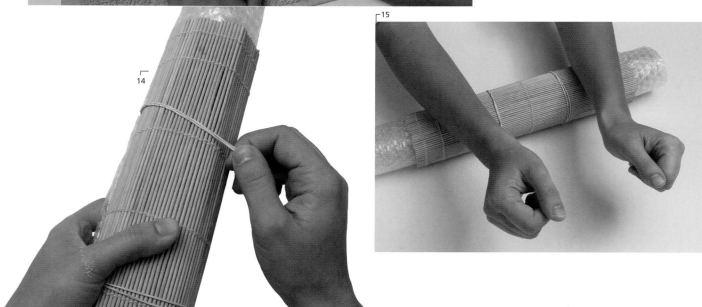

13- Put the felt tapestry back on the bubble wrap and roll it up with the roller.

14- Next, secure everything with rubber bands to prevent anything coming loose during the fulling process.

15- Roll the piece about fifty times, using all of your arms, from wrist to elbow.

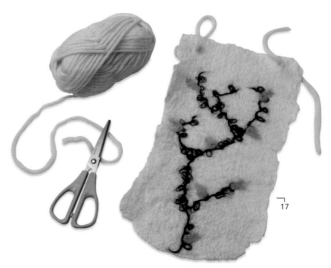

16- Unroll the tapestry to turn it over. Roll it up again and roll it fifty times on the other side.

17- Once the tapestry is dry, make two holes in the upper corners with scissors and knot two pieces of white wool through the holes so you can hang the piece.

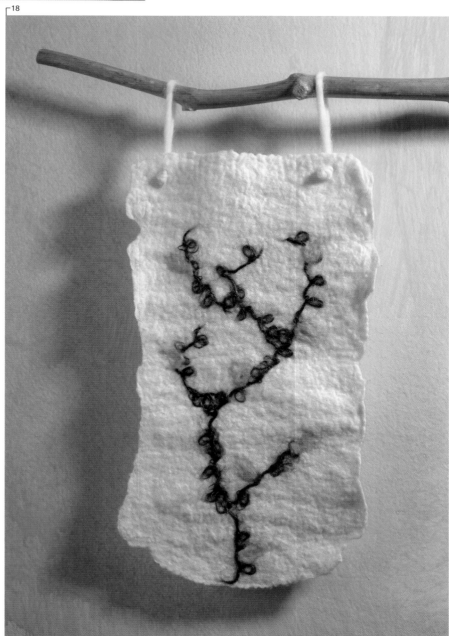

18- The felt tapestry is ideal for any little corner. Here the color of the flowers has been brought out by hanging the piece on a background of the same color.

Ladybugs for flowerpots

Show off your flowers and plants with some fun plant spikes decorated with felt ladybugs.

This project uses two felting techniques; soap and water to create the body of the bug so that it is very compact, and felting needles to add the details of the head and the characteristic spots of the ladybug. Using different techniques together will give you some surprising results and really attractive work.

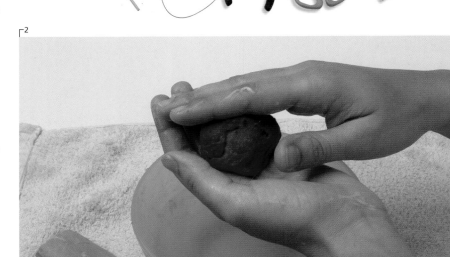

1- You will need a towel, red and black Merino wool, scissors, cutting pliers, fabric glue, a bar of mild soap, a wooden stick about 12" long, a spool of black 0.4-mm copper wire, a wool needle, a bowl with hot water, felting foam, individual felting needles, and a needle felting tool with a handle.

2- With the towel placed under your hands, make the red wool into a felt ball.

3,4 and **5-** Take the ball, which is approximately 1.5" in diameter, and slightly modify its shape by pressing with your fingers until it forms a body shape that is slightly flattened on the sides. Leave it to dry.

6- Place the red felt ball base on the felting foam, add a small amount of black wool and attach it using the needle felting tool. This will form the underside of the ladybug.

7- Next, go around the outline of this section using the individual felting needle.

8- Use this technique to add the head of the ladybug. Next, make a strand of black felt.

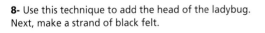

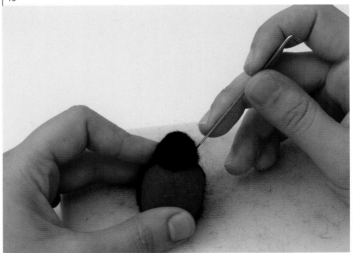

9- Now, add this strand around the head, fixing it with the individual needle.

10- This part will start to look like the head of a ladybug.

11 and **12-** Use another small strand of black wool to make the central line of the ladybug's body, jabbing it into the back from the head all the way down the body.

13- Attach the black spots of different sizes, which are so characteristic of ladybugs.

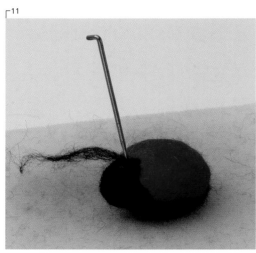

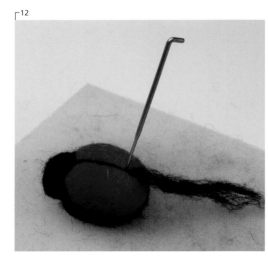

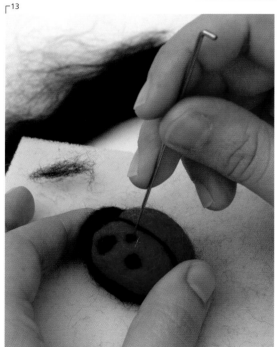

14- Make a hole in the ladybug's head with a wool needle in the place shown in the picture.

15- Carefully thread a piece of wire right through the hole so that it is poking out on both sides then, shape it with your fingers.

16- Use the scissors to make a cut in the shape of a cross in the stomach of the ladybug and push the sides of it inwards to make a hole.

17- Insert the tip of the tube of fabric glue into the hole and apply a few drop of glue.

18- Lastly, attach the wooden stick and leave to dry completely, as shown in the picture.

19- Make as many ladybugs, or any other bug, as you like to create a countryside feel to your balcony or terrace.

Table runner

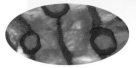

Next, you will learn how to make an extremely fine table runner using the cobweb technique. By adding colors and shapes with layers you can create an elegant design. This piece only uses a small amount of frayed wool to give a delicate, subtle look.

Bear in mind that pieces created using this technique should be used on surfaces that do not receive a great deal of wear and tear, in order to avoid your work getting damaged. You can also use this technique for making accessories.

2- Place the plastic bubble wrap over the bamboo mat. Next, take some frayed pieces of blue wool and lay them down along the bamboo mat.

3- Now, add some strands of green wool, laying them vertical to the blue wool, remembering to tease the strands out so that the piece does not become too matted.

4- Put the magenta wool in circles over some of the strands of green wool.

1- You will need a long bamboo mat, a piece of nylon mesh cloth, plastic bubble wrap, a roller, a long-handled brush, rubber bands, a bowl of very hot soapy water, and green, pink, magenta, and blue Merino wool.

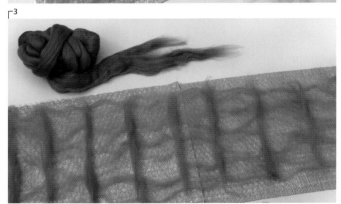

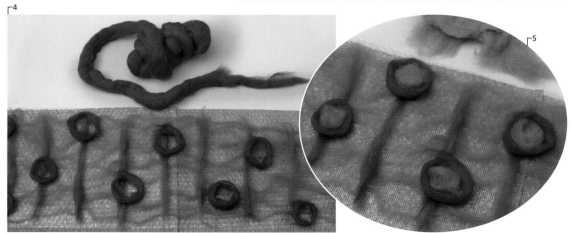

5- To finish off the design, fill the insides of the circles of magenta wool with pink wool.

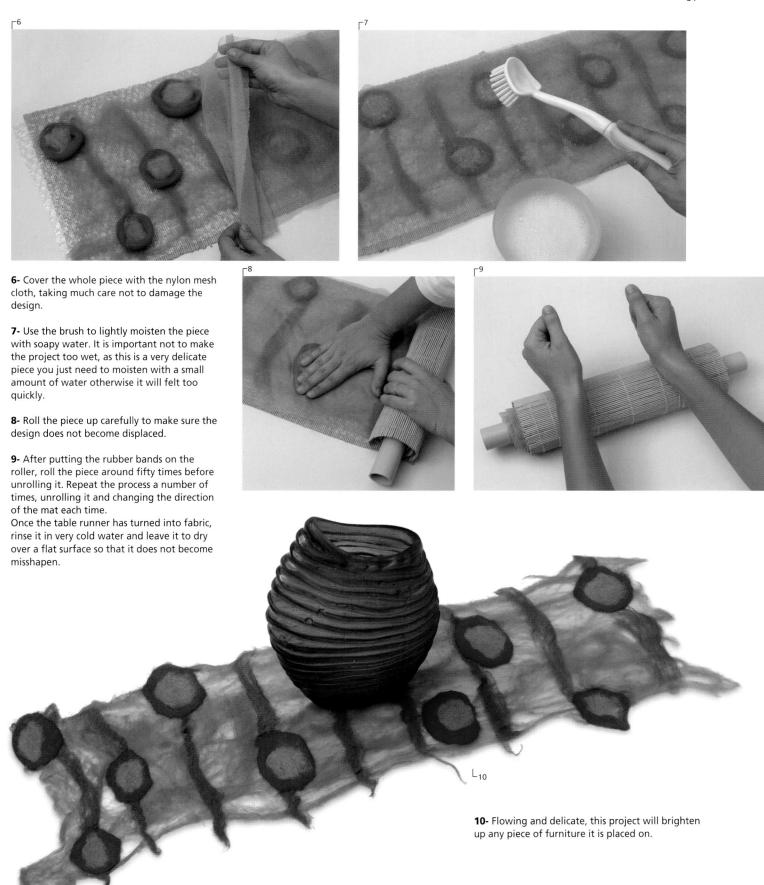

6- Cover the whole piece with the nylon mesh cloth, taking much care not to damage the design.

7- Use the brush to lightly moisten the piece with soapy water. It is important not to make the project too wet, as this is a very delicate piece you just need to moisten with a small amount of water otherwise it will felt too quickly.

8- Roll the piece up carefully to make sure the design does not become displaced.

9- After putting the rubber bands on the roller, roll the piece around fifty times before unrolling it. Repeat the process a number of times, unrolling it and changing the direction of the mat each time.
Once the table runner has turned into fabric, rinse it in very cold water and leave it to dry over a flat surface so that it does not become misshapen.

10- Flowing and delicate, this project will brighten up any piece of furniture it is placed on.

Vanity mirror

Wool can be used to cover all types of objects; these can be easy or difficult projects depending on their shape. The object chosen for this project is a small round vanity mirror, with a white polystyrene ball for the base. Both objects are easy to cover, as their size and shape are conducive to holding when felting.

To achieve a good finish you need to work patiently with your hands, as the larger the object, the longer it will take to felt.

1- For this project you will need purple and lilac colored Merino wool, a towel, plastic bubble wrap, nylon mesh cloth, a cutter, fabric glue, a polystyrene ball, a round mirror, a bowl filled with hot soapy water, a long-handled brush, and a round lid a little smaller than the mirror to use as a base.

2- Place the mirror reflective side up and put layers of purple wool on top, laying the fibers in alternate vertical and horizontal layers until you have two thick layers. Let some of the wool hang over the edges so you can tighten the felt later.

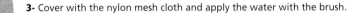

3- Cover with the nylon mesh cloth and apply the water with the brush.

4- Use a piece of the plastic bubble wrap to massage the wool, rubbing it in a circular motion until it has become a regular, even fabric.

5- Next, take off the nylon grid fabric and turn the project over, securing the excess felt on the edges by pulling it inwards on the mirror.

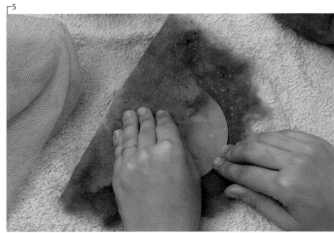

6- If necessary, add a little more purple wool in order to complete the back, this time without allowing any wool to hang over the edges.

7- Now repeat the massaging process with the plastic bubble wrap.

8- Once the felt has joined to the mirror inside it, properly rinse it. Remove any excess water with a towel or a paper towel if necessary.

9- Place the mirror with the side that you have worked on first face up (the reflective part of the mirror). Put the lid over the middle and cut around it with a cutter.

10- Now prepare the Polystyrene ball to be covered with the lilac colored wool.

11- Due to the size of the ball you will need to massage it a little more with your hands so that the felt joins the ball properly. Leave the two pieces you have created to dry.

12- Glue the ball onto the mirror with fabric glue.

13- This attractive mirror is ideal for decorating your dressing table. If you prefer, you can choose other geometric shapes for the base of your mirror.

Flower mobile

In the following exercise you will make some felted flowers that will be left semi-felted, or partially felted. The fulling process will be replaced by the use of some glue diluted in water, which will be added to each flower to stiffen them so that they appear to be fully felted. The flowers will be joined together with copper wire so they can be placed inside or outside.

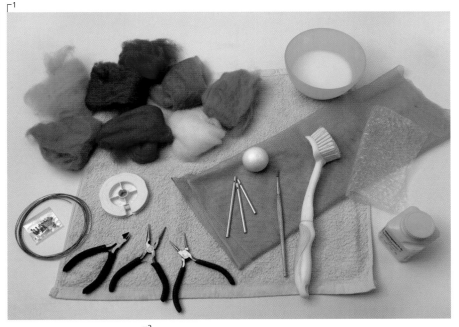

1- You will need magenta, white, purple, orange, green, lilac, blue, and pistachio-colored Merino wool, green 1-mm aluminum wire, round nose pliers, flat pliers, cutting pliers, 0.3-mm nylon wire, a sewing needle, crimp beads, metal rods for the mobile, a towel, plastic bubble wrap, a paintbrush, two bowls, one with hot soapy water, glue, a long-handled brush, nylon mesh fabric, and a Polystyrene ball.

2- Place the plastic bubble wrap on the towel, lay out some magenta wool, and spread some strands of white wool on top.

3- Place the nylon mesh fabric on top and, with the brush, wet the piece with hot soapy water.

4- Use a piece of plastic bubble wrap to massage the surface of the flower until the fibers join, but without them forming a compact fabric. Lift up the nylon fabric to check the progress of the fabric.

5- Extract the excess water with a towel or paper towel, put the flower back on the plastic bubble wrap, and use the brush to paint it with a little glue diluted in water.

6- Cut a piece of aluminum wire with the cutting pliers and roll it using the round nose pliers.

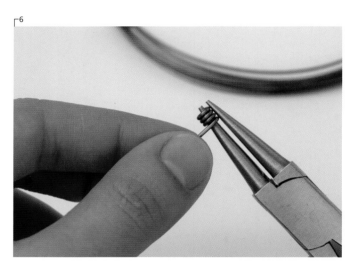

7- Insert the coil of wire through the decorated part of the flower.

8- Shape the flower with your hands and leave to dry. Here a plastic water bottle has been adapted by making two holes through it, which then support the wire while the flower dries.

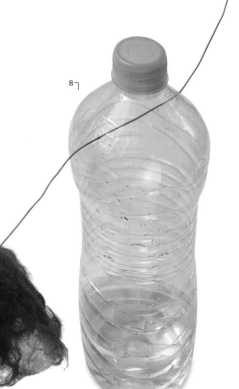

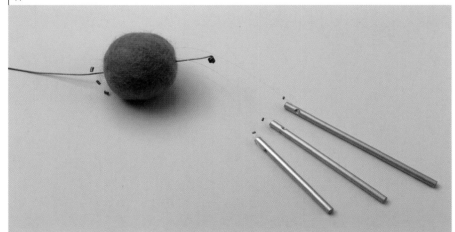

9- Cover the Polystyrene ball with green wool.

10- Use a sewing needle to thread three nylon wires through the ball, securing them with crimp beads so they do not fall out.

11- Insert a long piece of the coiled wire into the center of the ball. At each end of the nylon wire, add a metal rod for mobiles and secure with crimp beads.

12- Repeat the previous steps to create various flowers in different colored wool.

13- Once the pieces are dry, join them together by using the flat nose pliers to twist the pieces of wire from the flowers with the wire you have added to the green felt ball.

14- Leave a piece of wire to make a hook with which to hang the mobile.

15- This finished mobile looks bright and cheerful hanging anywhere in the house, from a window, a door, or even a mirror.

Sunflower bowl

You will now learn how to make a pleasing woolen bowl in the shape of a sunflower, and also see that it is possible to use other objects to obtain different shapes when working with felt. For this project you will use a plastic jar, ideal for making containers, and you will use the technique of directly massaging the wool with plastic bubble wrap in order to create the final shape. You will work with layers, as the piece needs to be hardwearing if it is to be used as a container. For this reason, you will have to apply a number of layers of wool and felt them well to achieve the shape and color of a sunflower.

1- You will need green, brown, and mustard-colored wool, a bamboo mat, a towel, plastic bubble wrap, rubber bands, a bowl of hot soapy water, a long-handled brush, nylon mesh fabric, a roller, and a plastic container.

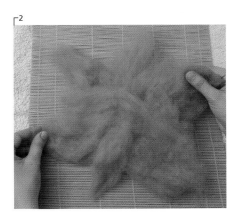

2- Place the bamboo mat on top of the towel and then lay out the mustard-colored wool, which will form the petals of the sunflower.

3- Add the brown and green wool.

4- Cover the flower with the nylon fabric and spread the hot soapy water over it with the brush.

5- Massage the flower with the corner of the plastic bubble wrap. Continue this process until you have achieved an even fabric.

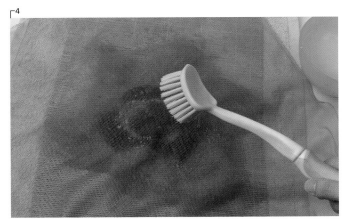

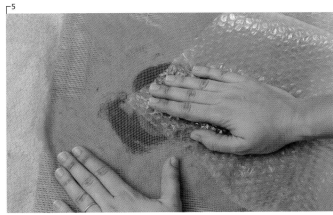

6- Carefully remove the nylon mesh fabric.

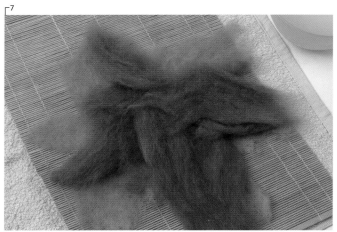

7- Turn over the fabric so you can complete the design on the back. Add the green wool, spreading it out to make the shape of leaves.

8- Cover the piece with the nylon fabric again, moisten it, and massage it with the help of the plastic bubble wrap.

9- After removing the nylon cloth, turn the flower over and cover it with the plastic bubble wrap, making sure the bubbles are face down to facilitate the fulling process.

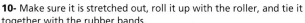

10- Make sure it is stretched out, roll it up with the roller, and tie it together with the rubber bands.

11- Roll the piece about fifty times. Repeat this process various times by unrolling the piece, turning the flower over and rolling it up again, and rolling another fifty times on the other side. You can do this about three or four times until you have a completely compact fabric.

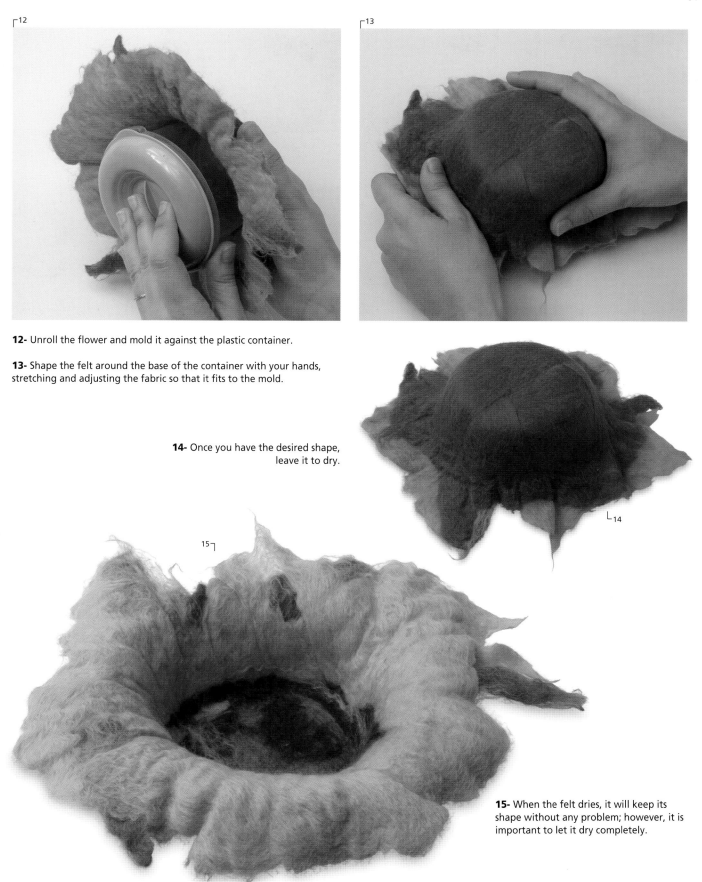

12- Unroll the flower and mold it against the plastic container.

13- Shape the felt around the base of the container with your hands, stretching and adjusting the fabric so that it fits to the mold.

14- Once you have the desired shape, leave it to dry.

15- When the felt dries, it will keep its shape without any problem; however, it is important to let it dry completely.

Variations

This section offers other possibilities for projects using felt designed for home décor.

You will see a series of pieces inspired by, or made in the same way as, the pieces in this chapter, as well as other alternatives.

The following pieces were made by Elvira Lopez del Prado, Ana Wingeyer, and Inger Maaike.

Tapestry wall-hanging with flower design. Felted with soap and water and decorated with needle felting.

Cute dragonfly spike for flower pot. Felted with needles.

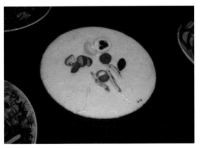

Mobile with bells for the front door. Mixed techniques: wet felting and needle felting.

Circular reversible tablecloth made using the cobweb technique.

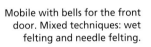

Fruits of the South. Ana Wingeyer, Argentina. Flavors and Languages exhibition, Antoni Miralda, 2007.

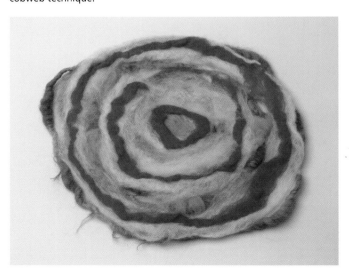

Vase-lamp. Inger Maaike Lutje Schipholt, Netherlands.

Jewelry box with lid. Felted with soap and water.

Picture frame.

Poppy and pansy shaped bowls.

Pillows made with commercially produced felt.

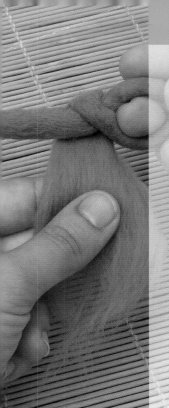

Felt and Accessories

In this last section of felt projects, the exercises start off easy and gradually become more difficult, with the most complex coming last. Throughout this section, you will use some of the techniques explained previously, but you will now apply them to different objects, combining pieces made with soap and water with those made with felting needles.

The pictures and examples shown here will serve as inspiration for creating your own designs.

Customizing clothes

Another way to use wool is to add it to a garment and felt it on using felting needles.

This is a very practical way to take advantage of left over colored wool, as well as rescue items from the back of your wardrobe that you no longer wear by giving them a new and original twist.

This technique works on most fabrics, except those which are particularly delicate.

1- For this project you will need a felting foam and an individual felting needle, some scissors, carded wool in a range of shades of blue, as well as yellow, orange, black, and bluish-gray carded wool.

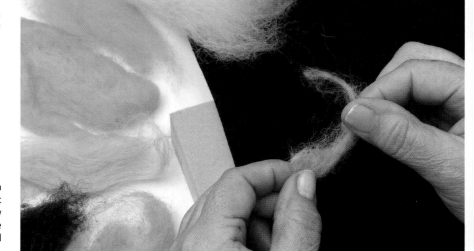

2- Here you will see how to decorate a black coat by felting the image of a sunset at sea. First, position some strands of yellow and orange wool mixed together. Use the needle to make the wool into the round shape of the sun.

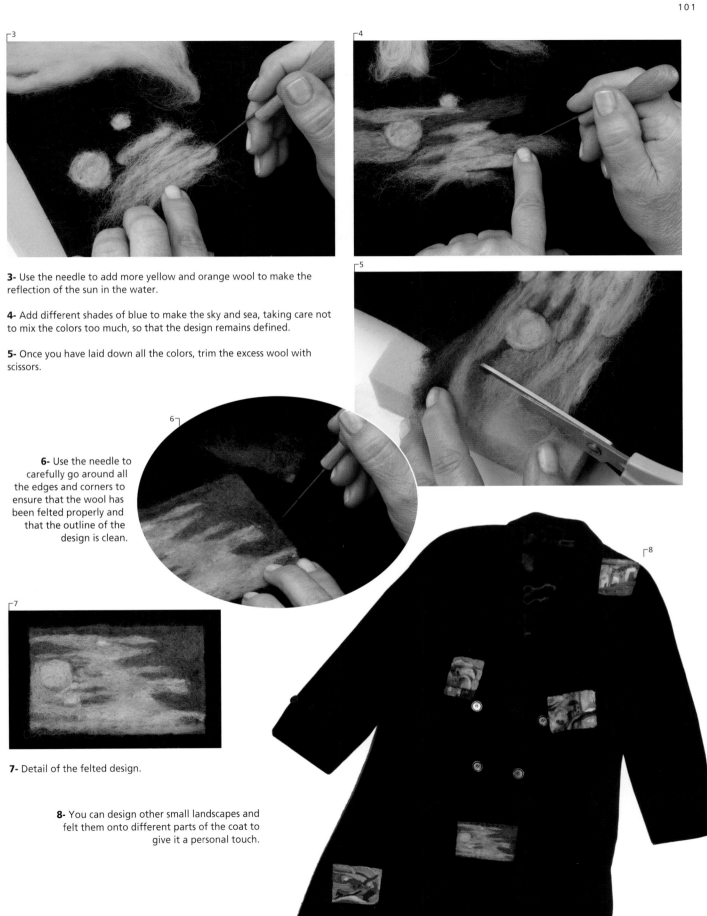

3- Use the needle to add more yellow and orange wool to make the reflection of the sun in the water.

4- Add different shades of blue to make the sky and sea, taking care not to mix the colors too much, so that the design remains defined.

5- Once you have laid down all the colors, trim the excess wool with scissors.

6- Use the needle to carefully go around all the edges and corners to ensure that the wool has been felted properly and that the outline of the design is clean.

7- Detail of the felted design.

8- You can design other small landscapes and felt them onto different parts of the coat to give it a personal touch.

Ring

You will now see how to make a colored ring, including the base, entirely from wool without the use of any other material.

For this project you will alternate between using wet felting and needle felting to achieve a more complex piece.

The felting process and the various tools used depend on the demands of the piece and also on the artist. Fulling is usually done with a roller and a bamboo mat, but in this case, you will be working directly with your hands due to the small size of the fabric.

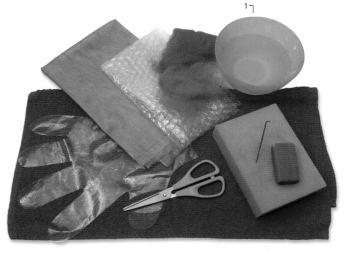

1- You will need blue and orange wool, a towel, plastic bubble wrap, a nylon mesh cloth, plastic gloves, a bowl of hot water, a bar of soap, a felting needle, scissors, and felting foam.

2- Lay out the towel on the work table and place the plastic bubble wrap on top. Pull the blue wool out into two layers and place one horizontally and one vertically.

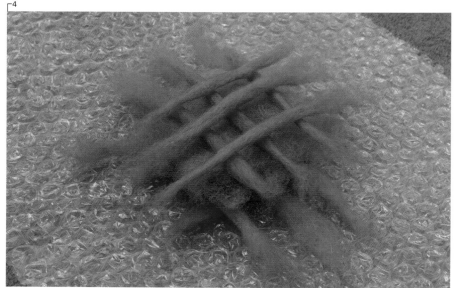

3- Take three strips of orange wool and place them vertically over the blue wool.

4- Put another three strips of orange wool horizontally over the other strips Turn the piece over, and repeat the process with the orange wool on the other side.

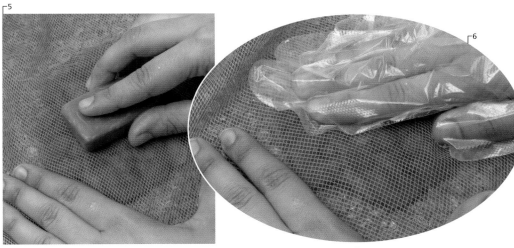

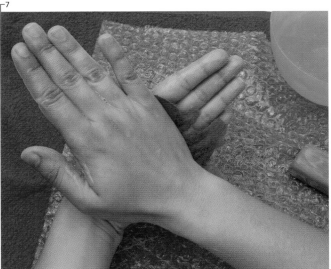

5- Place the nylon cloth over the pile of wool, wet it with hot water and rub with a bar of soap.

6- Wearing plastic gloves, massage until the fabric is completely felted.

7- With the fabric still wet and your hands lathered, begin the fulling process. Massage the felt vigorously, making circular movements with your hands so that the felt becomes well compacted.

8- Rinse well, and cut the felt into the shape of a circle with the scissors.

9- Make a small cord out of orange wool, wetting the middle part with soap and water and leaving the ends dry.

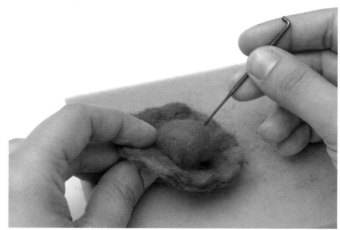

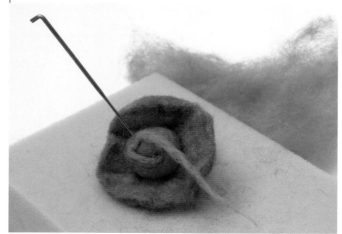

10- Use the scissors to make a small cut of about 5 mm in the center of the felt circle.

11- Introduce the ends of the orange cord through this hole, leaving out the felted part, which will become the band of the ring.

12- The next part is done with dry felting. Use the felting foam to rest the ring on, then use the needle to make the ends of the orange cord into the shape of a ball.

13- Lastly, use the felting needle to decorate the orange ball with a little of the blue wool.

14- While the ring dries, you can shape it as you wish. Once it is dry, you will be able to wear it without it becoming misshapen.

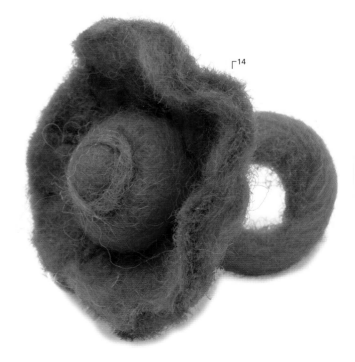

Net scarf

Once you have acquired enough skill working with felt and fulling, it is time to explore and experiment with new methods and shapes.

A case in point is the scarf featured here, which is designed to be worn for fashion rather than warmth due to its open structure. In this exercise, you will learn how to make pieces with a net design and large decorative spaces in a style that can be adapted to any garment or accessory. Felt is a very light material, meaning you can create a large yet lightweight scarf. You will use Merino wool so that the scarf feels delicate.

1- To felt your scarf you will need a towel, white, black, green, and turquoise Merino wool, plastic gloves, soapy water, rubber bands, a brush, a long piece of plastic bubble wrap, a very long bamboo mat (if necessary, you can sew two or three sewing mats together), a nylon mesh cloth, and a long, thin stick.

2- Lay the towel on the table, then put the bamboo mat and plastic bubble wrap on top. Arrange four strands of the green Merino wool vertically over the bubble wrap, leaving about 1.25" between each one. The length of your scarf will be determined by the length of these green wool strands. The wool will shrink by about 30%; therefore, for a scarf of about 1 m in length, lay out strands for 1.2 to 1.3 meters.

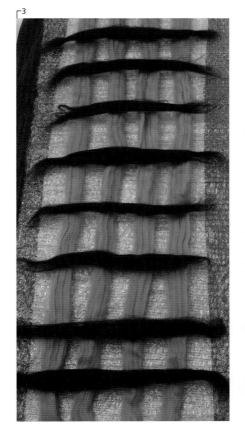

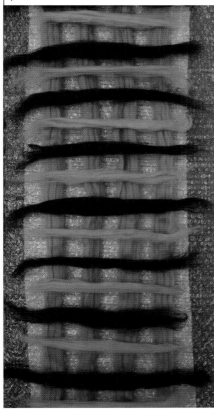

3- Arrange strands of black wool horizontally across the entire length of the scarf.

4- Add horizontal strands of turquoise-colored wool between the black strands.

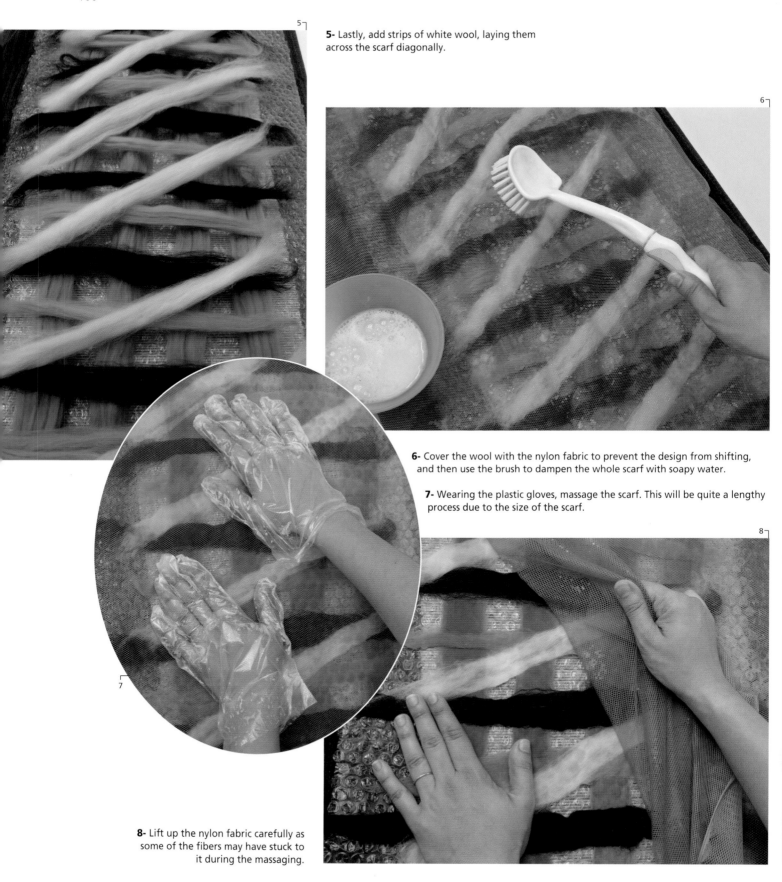

5- Lastly, add strips of white wool, laying them across the scarf diagonally.

6- Cover the wool with the nylon fabric to prevent the design from shifting, and then use the brush to dampen the whole scarf with soapy water.

7- Wearing the plastic gloves, massage the scarf. This will be quite a lengthy process due to the size of the scarf.

8- Lift up the nylon fabric carefully as some of the fibers may have stuck to it during the massaging.

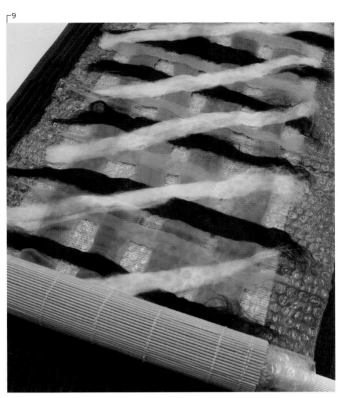

9- Position the stick and use it to roll up the piece. Keep the scarf stretched out as you roll to prevent the design from being damaged.

10- Secure the piece with the rubber bands and roll it about seventy times. Then unroll it, turn it over, and roll again another seventy times until you are sure that the fabric has been completely fulled.

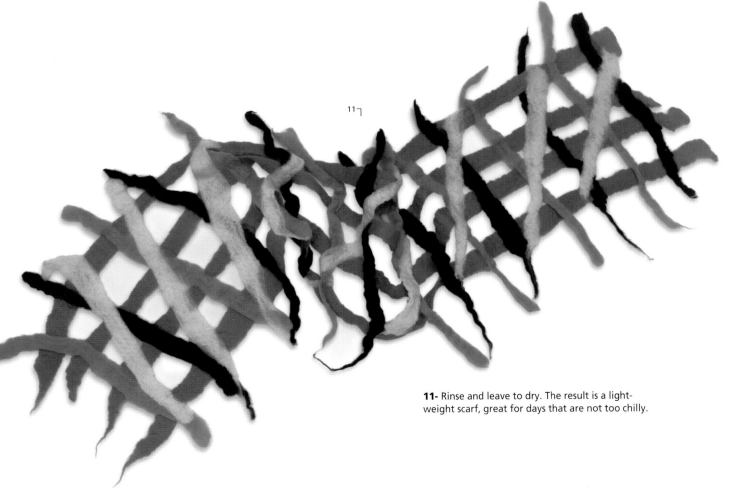

11- Rinse and leave to dry. The result is a light-weight scarf, great for days that are not too chilly.

Flower necklace

To make this piece of costume jewelry, you will again need to make a felt cord, but this time you will use it as the clasp of the necklace. You will work with flat shapes and shape them with your fingers, modeling them as if they were clay.

You will learn a different way of attaching flowers around a cord, using jewelry wire, beads, and crimp beads, and you will use a pair of pliers to finish the piece.

1- You will need a towel, plastic gloves, white, dark blue, turquoise, pink, and orange carded wool, green Merino wool, a bowl for hot water, a bamboo mat, a bar of soap, plastic bubble wrap, gold wire, nylon mesh fabric, a metal punch tool, cutting pliers, crimping pliers, a pair of scissors, pink, blue, green and orange rocaille beads, and some crimp beads.

2- Lay the towel on the work table and place the bamboo mat and plastic bubble wrap on top. Next, add two layers of white wool, one in a vertical direction and the other in a horizontal direction, and over this, place some strands of colored wool without mixing them.

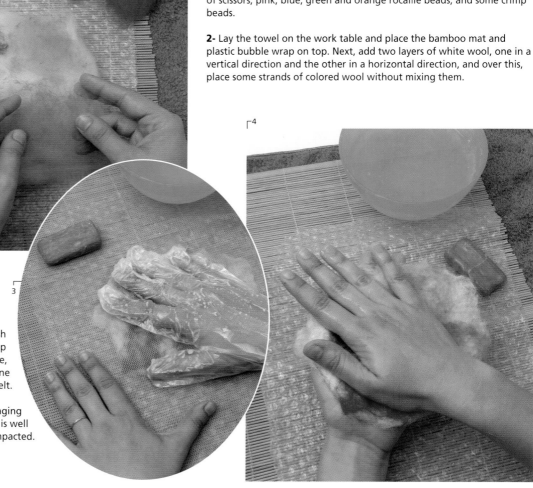

3- Cover with the nylon mesh fabric and wet with soap and water. Wearing a glove, massage the wool with one hand until it starts to felt.

4- Now start the fulling, massaging the fabric vigorously until it is well compacted.

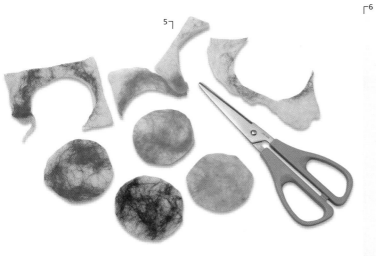

5- Rinse and cut each colored piece into a circle.

6- Cut each circle into the shape of a flower with six petals. With hot soapy water, mold the flowers and give them their shape by pushing your finger into their center and pushing the petals up around it. Rinse carefully and leave them to dry.

7- Make a cord with the green Merino wool by first wetting it with soapy water, and then rolling it inside the bamboo mat until the fabric becomes felted.

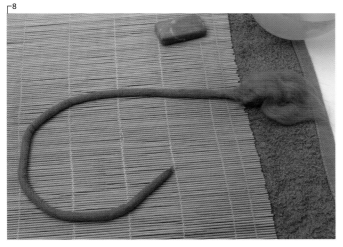

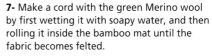

8- Leave the one end dry and unfelted.

9- To create a ring-shaped clasp, bend the dry unfelted end of the green cord in on itself, then roll it over the felted part of the cord.

10- Wet the clasp with soap and water and roll it in the bamboo mat, using enough force that both parts felt together.

11- Insert the cord through the ring and leave it like this to dry. After drying the flowers and lace, join them together.

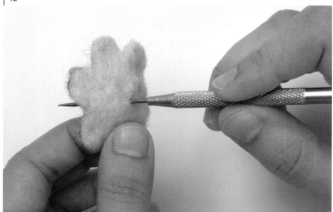

12- To join the flowers, make a hole in the center of each one with the punch.

13- Cut a piece of wire with the cutting pliers and thread one end through the hole in the center of the flower. Add a crimp bead and crimp it with the crimping pliers.

14- Add a few orange rocaille beads, place another crimp bead on the end, and then crimp it with the crimping pliers so that the beads do not come off the wire.

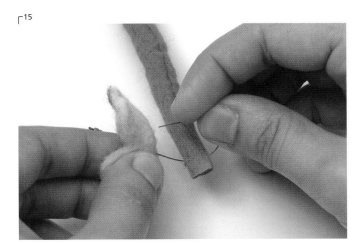

15- Attach the flower to the green cord by first looping the wire around the cord and then inserting it into the hole in the flower.

16- Repeat the process of adding a crimp bead, crimping it with pliers, adding a few rocaille beads before adding another crimp bead, and fixing it with the crimping pliers. Cut off the excess wire.

17- Follow these steps for the other flowers and arrange them to your liking along the cord. To open and close the necklace, you can pass the flowers through the ring clasp or you can make the cord the right the size to fit over your head so that you can just put the necklace on and off without having to use the felt ring clasp.

Purse

You will now make a practical bag with handles, perfect for an autumn or winter evening. For this piece you will use flat, commercially produced felt rather than wool.

The flat felt is approximately 0.25" thick, and you will need to use a sewing machine to finish the piece off and an iron to attach the flower decorations.

You will need to have basic knowledge of how to use a sewing machine to join the pieces of felt together and for the decorative zigzag pattern.

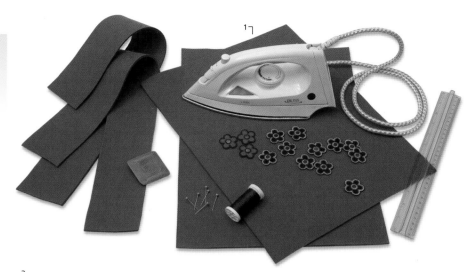

1- You will need two 12" x 16" flat, rectangular felt sheets in lilac for the body of the purse, two 24" x 3" strips of the same felt for the handles, various iron-on flower decorations, a ruler, tailor's chalk, purple thread, some pins, and an iron.

2- Using tailor's chalk, draw the design with the bough of flowers onto the two pieces of felt that will be the body of the bag.

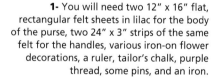

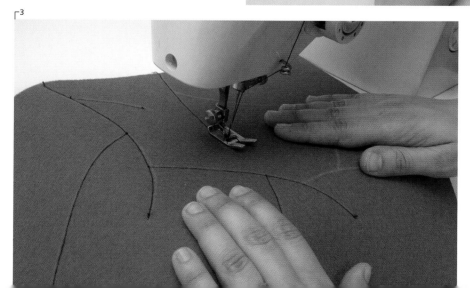

3- With the sewing machine, sew a zigzag pattern over the design with purple thread. Do the same thing on the other piece of felt.

4- Next, position the flowers in your chosen design onto the felt and then iron them on in order to fix them onto the fabric.

5- Take the 24" x 3" strips of felt and vertically fold them down the middle, marking them with a ruler and fastening them with pins. Leave a distance of about 2.5" at each end.

6- Now sew the strips of felt with the sewing machine, keeping to the margins you have marked.

7- Place a handle over one part of the purse, and pin it 2" from each end.

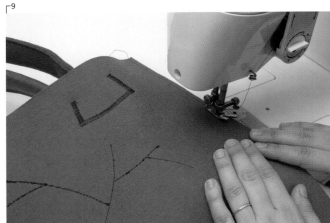

8- With the sewing machine sew a zigzag pattern as decoration, following the outline of the end of the handle. Do the same for each of the ends of the handles.

9- With the sewing machine sew both sides of the purse together, beginning on one side and finishing on the opposite side to form a "u." Leave the fourth side unsewn for the opening of the purse.

10- So that the purse can stand up on its own without falling over, sew across the inside bottom corners to make triangles, which create a base for the purse.

11- Turn the bag right side out, leaving the seams on the inside. It will now stand up thanks to the little sewing trick from the last step. Your purse is now ready to use.

Nuno
spring scarf

You will now see how to make a scarf especially designed for spring made from a very lightweight silk fabric with only the ends felted. Using an extremely delicate technique called *nuno* felting, which requires working on the wool with cold water so that the felting process takes place slowly and allows the wool to felt onto the silk, you will get very elegant results.

For the project, choose any kind of silk or lightweight fabric, provided it has an open weave that allows the woolen fiber to penetrate the fabric and form felt.

Part of the decoration for the scarf uses white Merino wool that has previously been blended with silk; this will give a lustrous and very delicate look to the piece.

1- You will use a foam rubber tube (or something that serves the same purpose), a container for the soap and water, rubber bands, a bamboo mat, plastic bubble wrap, nylon mesh fabric, Merino wool in various colors, white Merino wool blended with silk, a sponge, a towel, and a chiffon or silk gauze scarf.

2- Dissolve the soap flakes in cold water, lay out the plastic bubble wrap, and place the silk fabric on top. On top of the fabric lay a small amount of wool with the fibers loosely frayed.

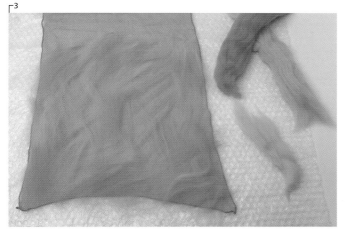

3- Cover the fabric with a layer of mustard, yellow, and peach Merino wool.

4- Make a flower with the silk-blended wool, positioning the strands as shown in the photograph. Also add a few small strands of mustard and brown Merino wool to the design for decoration.

5- Decorate a little more by adding colored wool until the design of the flower is complete. This is the complete design that the scarf will have at both ends. The wool blended with silk gives a nice sheen to the flower.

6 and **7-** Cover the design with the nylon mesh fabric, wet with a sponge dampened with soap and cold water and begin to massage with your hands.

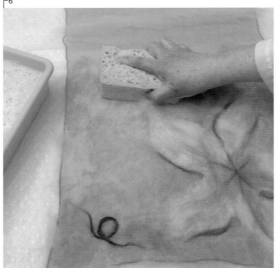

8- Once the design has fixed to the scarf and will not shift, remove the nylon mesh cloth.

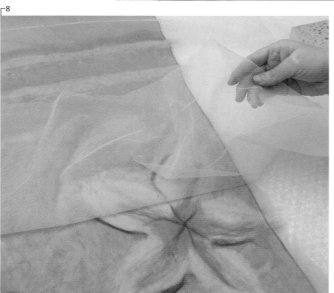

9- Use the foam rubber tube to roll up the part of the fabric with the flower design.

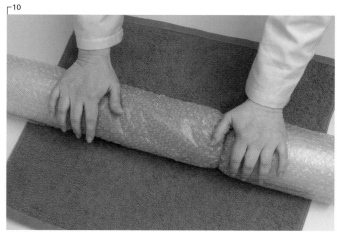

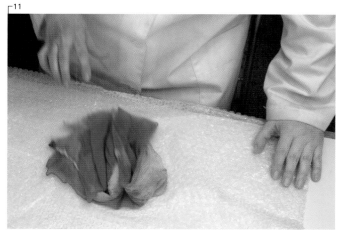

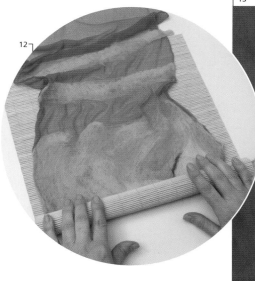

10- Use the rubber bands to secure the piece so that the silk does not move. Roll the piece on a towel around two hundred times on each side.

11- Take out the scarf, rinse it, fold it and beat it hard over the work table. Now you can begin the fulling process.

12- Next, roll the scarf directly with the bamboo mat so that the wool becomes more matted, and then roll it around twenty-five times. If the fabric has still not compacted properly, repeat the process. Do the same thing on the other side of the scarf.

13- Here we have the result: a beautiful spring scarf.

Shibori beret

The shibori technique comes from Japan and consists of dyeing fabric that has been knotted and folded to create textures. This technique has since spread to the knitting world, where small objects (for example, dried fruits) are wrapped up in different parts of a garment knitted in 100% wool. These objects are held in place by rubber bands and felted in that position, in this case using the washing machine, resulting in unique pieces.

This project's main difficulty lies in the technique of using four needles for knitting; it is therefore advisable to have some basic knowledge of the technique.

Working with four needles is common for making circular shapes, such as hats, socks and gloves, and is very practical, as it reduces the amount of work needed to make a garment, in this case a beret. Start off in rib (two knit stitches and two purl stitches) and knit about 0.75". Knit the rest of the beret in stockinette (plain) stitch which, as you are working in a circular motion, is all knit stitch on the right side in the same direction.

It is a good idea to make a 4" x 4" sample square and then felt it in the washing machine, so as to know how much shrinkage will occur, and therefore, how many stitches you will have to cast on.

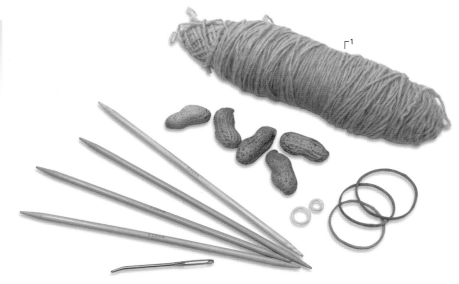

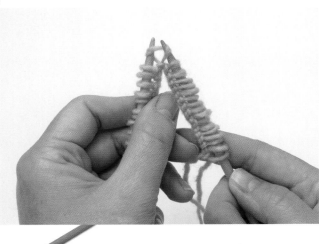

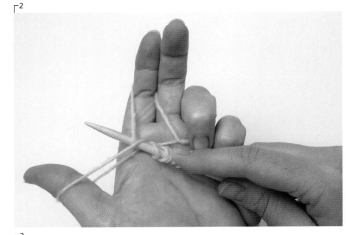

1- You will need a ball of Worsted 100% wool, four 5-mm double-pointed needles, a wool sewing needle, rubber bands, some peanuts (or dried fruit), some markers (optional), and a washing machine for the felting process.

2- Cast on eighty-eight stitches onto one of the needles.

3- Divide the stitches out evenly over three of the four needles.

4- Once spread out, the stitches will look like this. Now you are ready to start knitting.

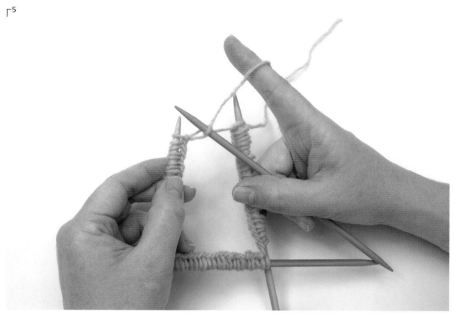

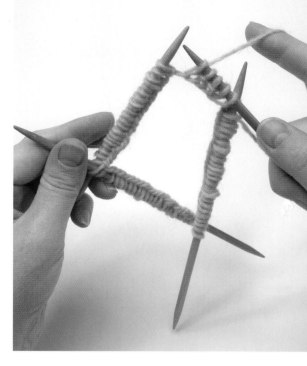

5- Join, taking care that the stitches are not twisted.

6- Commence knitting, using the fourth knitting needle to knit off each of the other three needles in turn in a circular fashion.

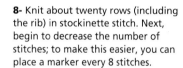

7- This is what the piece will look like when you have knitted the rib.

8- Knit about twenty rows (including the rib) in stockinette stitch. Next, begin to decrease the number of stitches; to make this easier, you can place a marker every 8 stitches.

9- Knit one row decreasing a stitch and one row without decreasing. To decrease, knit two stitches together with the fourth needle.

10- To finish off decreasing the stitches, thread the wool needle with a piece of wool and pass it through all the stitches to take them off the needles. This also closes the beret.

11- To finish off the beret sew around the hole and cut the thread. Now you can tackle the shibori technique: start off by putting a peanut inside the beret and pulling the fabric tightly around it.

12- Use a rubber band to keep the peanut in place, making sure it is very tight to prevent it falling out during the felting process in the washing machine. Once all the peanuts are secured in the hat, put it in the washing machine and select a hot wash program (104° F) without pre-wash. When you take the piece out of the washing machine, remove the peanuts and rubber bands.

13- Once dry, you will have a fun, ethnic looking beret.

Seamless shoulder bag

This piece is made from Merino wool in various colors. It is a good idea to weigh or measure the wool when the project calls for specific amounts.

This piece requires 3 oz. of green wool and the same quantity of navy blue wool, with another 1 oz. of wool in each color to make the handles of the bag.

Another way to check that there is the same amount of each color is to measure the length of the wool.

The pattern for this bag will be a square of plastic bubble wrap.

1- You will need navy blue, green, yellow, and orange Merino wool, a towel, a felt-tip pen, scissors, a needle and thread for sewing, a plastic container with hot water, a sponge, a bar of mild soap, a roller padded with bubble wrap, two pieces of nylon mesh cloth, plastic bubble wrap, and a cardboard packet.

2- Separate the amount of wool needed for the bag and the handle: 3 oz. of each color for the bag and 1 oz. of each color for the handles.

3- Put the plastic bubble wrap on top of the towel. Then, place the additional piece of plastic bubble wrap, which will serve as the pattern, on top; mark this a few inches from the edge to indicate where the flap will be. On top of these, place the nylon mesh cloth, and then add small pieces of the green wool in vertical layers to make up this side of the bag.

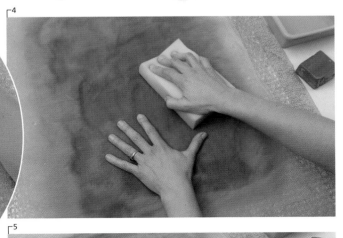

4- This part of the bag includes what will be the flap. Repeat the previous process, but this time place pieces of green wool horizontally. Next, flatten them with your hands to remove all the air in the fibers.

By this point, you will have used 1.5 oz. of wool. Now, cover everything with the nylon mesh cloth, and use a sponge to soak it all, except for the edges.

5- Put soap all over the surface and massage with your hands, rubbing until the cloth becomes compact.

6- Remove the nylon mesh cloth and lift up the plastic pattern that you placed over the surface of the bag. Fold all the edges inwards towards the marker line.

7- Place some strands of wool in a horizontal layer and then a vertical layer up to the marker line.

8- Put the nylon mesh cloth on top and rub over with soap and water.

9- Turn the piece over, wet the edges, and turn inwards.

10- Add a navy wool coat horizontally, place the nylon mesh on top, moisten with water and soap, and massage it with your hands to flatten and bind the fibers.

11- Go around the whole project. Turn the blue wool edges inward to the marker of the flap.

12- You have just covered part of the bag with a layer of blue wool laid horizontally, so now, cover the surface with the nylon mesh cloth again, and once again apply more soap and water and massage the piece with your hands.

13- Turn the piece over again. Again, work the edges inwards, wet and soap them again, and massage the piece with the help of the nylon cloth.

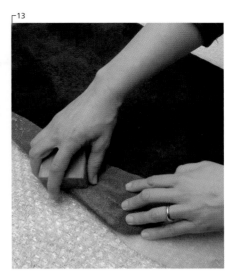

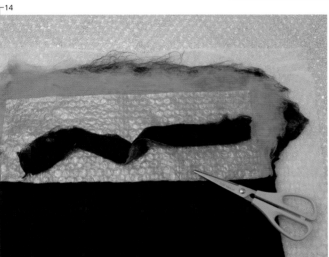

14 and **15-** Turn the project once again. With scissors cut off a strip and remove the plastic bubble wrap a little from inside so you can massage the edge and make it even.

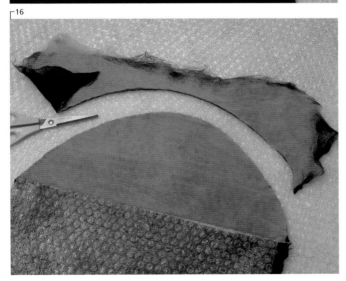

16- Cut the top flap by eyeballing it, then massage the edge so it is well defined.

17- Leaving the plastic bubble wrap pattern inside, roll up the bag and roll it about fifty times with the roller before taking it out. Repeat the process for both sides of the bag.

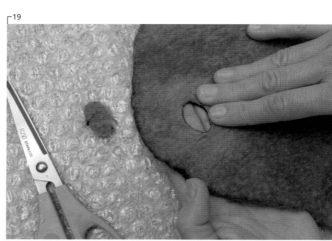

18 and **19-** Rinse the piece with water to eliminate the soap residue. Put the cardboard packet into the bag to help shape the bag, and leave to dry completely. Make a small hole with scissors for the clasp of the bag, and work it a little with your fingers to shape the edges.

20- To make the handle of the shoulder bag felt a 8 in. x 20 in. section of wool in two colors following the process explained at the beginning of this project.
Once it has been fulled, cut the strap in three equal pieces, sew them together, and join the handle to the ends of the bag.

21- To finish the piece off, sew a yellow and orange felt flower (as made in Chapter 3 of this book) to the body of the bag; this will go through the hole in the flap and act as a clasp.

Slippers

You are now going to make some colorful house slippers using only wool. This material will make them warm and comfortable, like socks. You will learn how to give them the shape of the right or left foot as needed, and how to make them just the right size. For this, you will need to draw a paper template of the bottom of your foot, adding around 25% to account for shrinkage. You will then transfer this pattern to plastic bubble wrap. If you prefer, you may use stiff or foam cardboard for the pattern, or even shoe lasts. Whilst working on these slippers, you will use your feet as the mold.

1- The materials needed to make two medium size slippers are yellow and orange Merino wool, 3 oz. of white Merino wool (1.5 oz. for each slipper), a bamboo mat, scissors, a ruler, a pen, plastic bubble wrap, a towel, a bowl for water, a bar of soap, a sponge, a piece of nylon mesh cloth, a foot template, and the corresponding template in plastic bubble wrap, cut 25% larger.

2- Lay down the towel, the plastic bubble wrap, and the plastic bubble wrap template, and on top of these, add some 0.75 oz. of white wool in two layers, one vertical and one horizontal.

3- Cover with the nylon cloth and use a wet soapy sponge to wet the piece all over, except the edges.

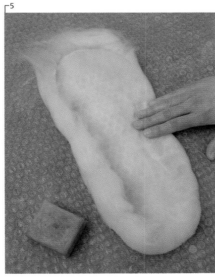

4- Turn the piece over, fold the edges inwards, and dampen.

5- Repeat the process. Add another 0.75 oz. of the white wool to create the other part of the slipper; add it in two layers, one vertical and one horizontal. Cover it with the nylon mesh cloth and dampen the piece as you work, leaving the edges dry. Turn the piece over once more and work the edges, dampening them and massaging them towards the inside of the slipper. Cover with the nylon cloth and massage everything until it is firm and compact.

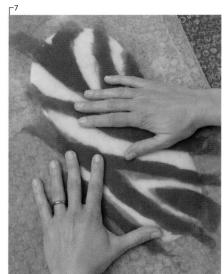

6- Pre-felt a piece of fabric (see Chapter 3) with two colors of wool—yellow and orange. Cut various irregular strips of different shapes with scissors, and place them over the slipper.

7- Put the nylon cloth on top and work the fabric, dampening it with soap and water until all is meshed together.

8- Turn the slipper over and work on the other side so that the added strips are joined in properly.

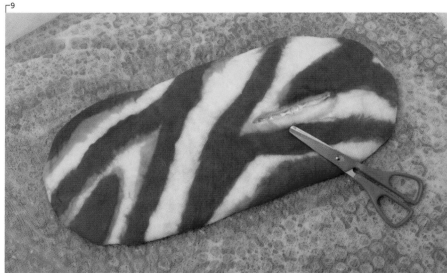

9- Leaving a space of about three fingers' width from the heel, cut an opening of about 4 in. with the scissors and take out the template from inside the slipper. Work the edges around the opening so they become well defined.

10- Continue working with your hands, massaging the body of the slipper so the fabric becomes better felted.

11- Now, roll the slipper in the bamboo mat and roll it, as before, in all directions; about sixty times per side.

12- Rinse well and drain the water. Put on the shoe and fit the opening to the shape of your foot.

13- Continue working on the slipper whilst wearing it to give it the shape of your right or left foot. By doing this you can make it fit your foot perfectly. Leave it to dry. Repeat the same process for each slipper.

14- Here, the decoration of the left slipper is going in a different direction, giving the slippers a quirky and unconventional touch. Your slippers are now ready to wear.

Seamless cap

In the following project, you will learn how to make a seamless cap. You use a pattern made of plastic bubble wrap, onto which you mark a circle about 12 in. in diameter, suitable for an average-sized head. However, you can change the size according to your needs.

Use a female polystyrene head to complete the final massage for the piece, and as a place to leave the cap to dry and take on the shape of a head.

You will felt the wool with soap and water, alternating between hot water with dissolved soap flakes and a bar of soap, to facilitate the work of massaging with your hands.

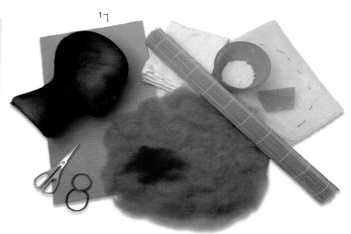

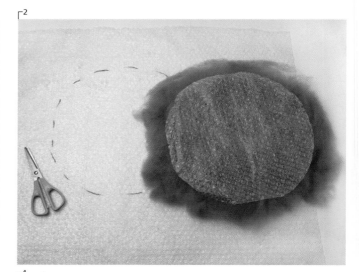

1- You are going to need a pair of scissors, a bowl of soap flakes dissolved in very hot water, a bar of soap, rubber bands, a large bamboo beach mat, a Polystyrene head, a pattern made from plastic bubble wrap, light and dark blue wool, a towel, and a textured rubber towel to aid the felting process.

2- Lay out the marked pattern, and on top of this add the light blue wool in two layers, one laid horizontally and one vertically, leaving about 1.5 in. sticking out along the edges of the outline. Cut another plastic circle the same size and place it on top of the wool; this will show you which part you need to moisten.

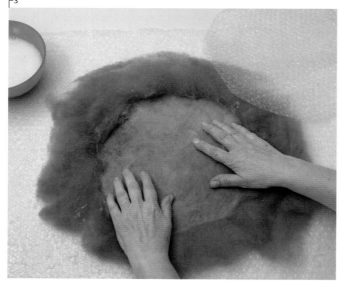

3- Remove the plastic circle and wet the central part of the wool with the hot, soapy water; lathering your hands with soap will make massaging easier.

4- Place the pattern from underneath on top of the wool. Add light blue wool to make two layers, one horizontal and one vertical.

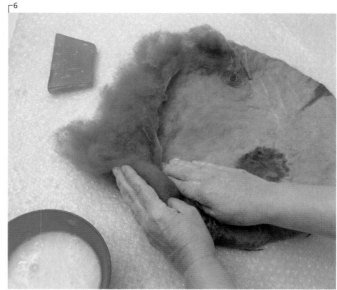

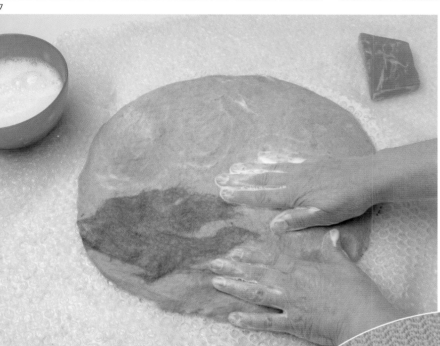

5- For decoration, add a small amount of dark blue wool.

6- Dampen the edges and fold them back inwards towards the center, massaging the whole piece so that it felts. By doing this, the inner and outer circles will felt at the same time, avoiding the need for seams so that the cap is made out of just one piece of felt.

7- Massage both sides, turning the fabric over until the first felting takes place.

8- With a small piece of dark blue wool, make a decoration for the cap. Wet it and roll it over the textured foam mat, leaving one end dry and unfelted.

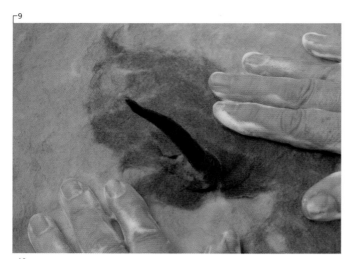

9- Join the decoration to the cap by wetting the dry part and massaging it into the cap with soap and water.

10- Lay the towel on top of the bamboo mat, fold it over with the cap in the middle, and roll everything together.

11- Either secure the mat with rubber bands or roll the bamboo mat over the textured foam mat to prevent it from slipping. Roll each side fifty times.

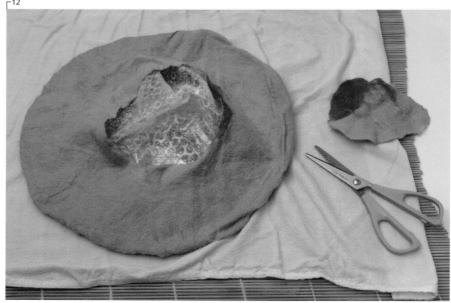

12- Cut a circle with scissors and remove the pattern.

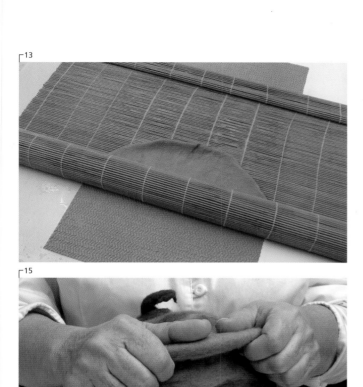

13- Move on to the fulling process. Put the cap inside the bamboo mat without the towel and roll it up, then roll it another fifty times per side, pressing down hard.

14- Remove the cap from the bamboo mat. Put one hand on the inside the cap, and use your other hand to massage and shape the material on the sides. Full the felt more if necessary and then rinse with cold water.

15- Put the cap over the Polystyrene head and massage it again hard, until it takes on the right shape. Leave it to dry on the head.

16- Once dry, your cap is ready to use on cold winter days.

Variations

Next, you will see a series of felt pieces created by artists and artisans from around the world.

These accessories have been decorated using the techniques explained in the projects in this section and include necklaces, purses, caps, rings, slippers, and also garments felted with a washing machine.

Felt cord necklace. María Ribeiro, Portugal.

Ring created by knotting around a woolen cord. Elvira López del Prado, Spain.

Child's jersey made using the shibori felting technique. All You Knit Is Love, Spain.

Nuno shawl. Mercé Puig, Spain.

Cap. María Jesús Fernández, Spain.

"Collar" made with the net felting technique. María Jesús Fernández, Spain.

Felt baby shoes. María Ribeiro, Portugal.

Necklace made with felted wool. María Jesús Fernández, Spain.

Customized jacket. María Jesús Fernández, Spain.

Artists' gallery

In the following pages are photographs showing the work of artists from all over the world who work with felt. We showcase a great variety of pieces, all created using the techniques covered in the projects in this book (wet felting, dry felting, and working with flat felt).

The aim of this gallery is to serve as an inspiration for your future felt creations as well as to show the wide range of possibilities that can be made using felted wool.

Necklace with felt balls. María Ribeiro, Portugal.

Breakfast at Tiffany's sleep masks. Claudia Costa Pedret, Spain.

Backpack. Elvira López del Prado Rivas, Spain.

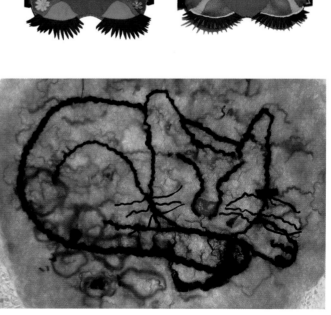

Kiali (detail). Ana Wingeyer, Argentina.

Gnome. Mercé Puig, Spain.

Red coat from the "Princesses" collection, nuno technique. Nuria "Nuna" Conesa, Spain. Photographs by Pablo Orcajo.

Chocolate and strawberry ring. Isabel Buesa Garcés, Spain.

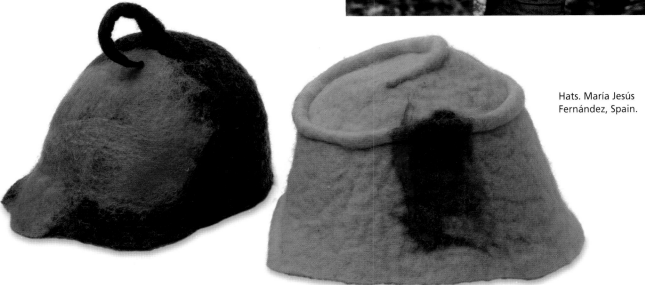

Hats. María Jesús Fernández, Spain.

Sheep. Mercé Puig, Spain.

Handbag. María Dolores
García, Spain.

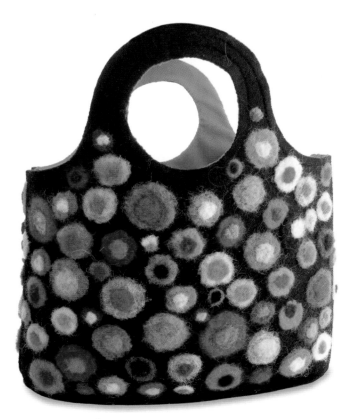

Princess Rose feeding
a dove. Alexandra
Kaczmarek, Poland.

Two Ladybugs in Love. Natalie
Kalinova, Australia.

Felt fascinator. Cristina Vásquez, Spain.

Pendant. Àngels Cordón, Spain.

America necklace. María Rebeca
Seisdedos, Chile.

Autumn cottages. Elisa Castro, Spain.

"Forest" suit jacket collection in the nuno technique. Nuria "Nuna" Conesa, Spain. Photography by Paul Orcajo.

Teacup pincushions made from recycled, felted jerseys. Betz White, United States.

Colored felt ring. Isabel Buesa Garcés, Spain.

Nuno scarf. Beth Connors, United Kingdom.

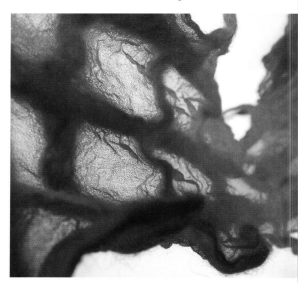

Booties. Ana Rodríguez
Ochagavía, Spain.

Africa Necklace. Elvira López del Prado, Spain.

Purse in fuchsia felt.
Mariví Ricart, Spain.

Nuno scarf. María Jesús Fernández, Spain.

Collage necklace. María Rebeca
Seisdedos, Chile.

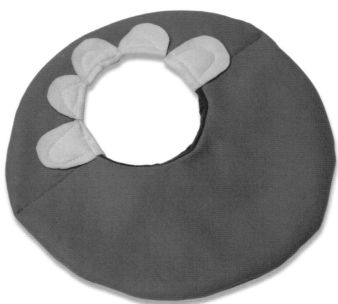

Daisy purse. Elvira López del Prado, Spain.

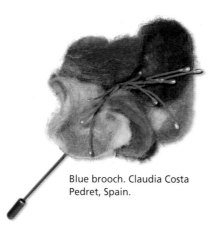

Blue brooch. Claudia Costa
Pedret, Spain.

Car decorations. Isabel Buesa Narro, Spain.

Felted flowers decoration. Isabel Martínez Narro, Spain.

Bird purses with zippers. Betz White, United States.

Brazil, necklace. Elvira López del Prado, Spain.

Boots. María Jesús Fernández, Spain.

Glossary

Bamboo mat
Table or beach mat made from bamboo. These are used because bamboo cane is rounded, which facilitates the process of massaging the wool, for example, when making cords.

Carding wool
Process of passing the wool fibers between two cylinders with spikes to eliminate remains of vegetation trapped in the wool; also helps to make all the fibers go in the same direction. This process is often completed industrially, but it is also possible to do it by hand with hand carders or by using a special tool called a drum carder. Carding wool also allows for the mixing of colors, once the fibers have been dyed.

Cobweb
Technique involving felting small quantities of wool. The final effect is a see-through fabric rather like a spider's web.

Combing wool
Process by which a series of fine combs are passed through wool to prepare the fibers, making them lie in a parallel fashion in order to remove short fibers.

Cotton
Thread or fabric of vegetable origin that is used for making garments and accessories.

Eva foam
Hard, dense foam commonly used as a base for felting with needles in order to prevent the tips of the needles breaking.

Fabric
Result of interlacing fibers in order to create garments.

Felt
Non-woven material resulting from stressing wool fibers until they become compacted.

Felting
Process through which wool fibers are permanently pressed together, thus creating a fabric called felt. This can be done by using various methods, including a wet process using mild soap and hot water, or through a dry process using felting needles and felting bases.

Felting needles
Special metal needles that consist of a thin handle and a barbed pointed end that is repeatedly jabbed into the woolen fibers to felt them.

Fiber
Filaments of animal or vegetable origin that form part of the composition of fabrics.

Flat felt
The name given to the fabric sold in specialist stores that has been commercially produced with industrial felting methods.

Friction
Result of massaging wool fibers, using one's hands or another object, so that they felt together.

Fulling
The second part of the felting process, consisting of beating and hitting the woolen fabric in order to compress and compact the fibers.

Layers
Pieces of woolen fiber placed one on top of another in order to create thickness or volume.

Lightweight
Used to describe fabric that is not heavy. One of felt's characteristics is its lightness.

*M*assaging
Pressing or rubbing wool fibers hard in order to create felted fabric.

Merino
Type of sheep, originally from Spain, whose wool is of especially high quality. Silky to the touch and lustrous in appearance, it is widely used for felting when making clothing and accessories.

Metal cutters
Shaped similar to those used to cut homemade cookie dough. These cutters are used to make wool decorations for needle felting.

Mild soap
Alkaline-free soap with no perfume or colorants

Mongols
Ethnic tribes that used to occupy modern-day Mongolia and its hinterlands; they have been credited with the discovery of felt.

*N*uno
Japanese word for fabric. In terms of felting, it is the name given to a technique where wool is felted over a lightweight fabric, such as silk or gauze, to create unique folds and textures.

Nylon mesh cloth
Synthetic material used in the felting process. It is placed over wool to prevent the fibers from shifting during the massaging process.

*P*attern
A shape or template cut from paper or other material that is placed on top of felted fabric in order to obtain a piece the same shape and size.

Pazyryk culture
Culture pertaining to the Pazyryk people—nomadic horsemen who lived on the Russian steppes 2,500 years ago and engaged in war, hunting, and grazing animals. Many felted works from their era have been preserved.

Plastic bubble wrap
Used to massage wool by pressing the air bubbles against it, which then helps the felting process.

*R*oller
Long, rounded tool made of any material that is used to roll the felt, which has been rolled up around it during the fulling process.

Rolling
Action of moving the felting roller backwards and forwards. These movements are usually carried out with a bamboo mat rolled up around the roller.

Rubber band
Strip of rubber or elastic material that is used in felting work to hold the bamboo mat and roller in place during the fulling process or when felting the wool.

*S*heer
Fine, lightweight fabric; for example, silks and gauzes.

Shibori
Japanese technique that involves creating folds in fabric so that textures are created during dyeing. Certain areas of the wool garment are stretched around small objects and then secured with rubber bands to create shapes. Once the garment has been completely felted, the rubber bands and objects are removed and the shapes remain in the fabric.

Soap flakes
Soap can be bought in flake form. This format is useful, as it dissolves directly into water without disrupting the felting process and sidesteps having to rub the piece with a bar of soap.

Strands
Name given to the fibers of wool or any other textile material. These can be teased apart, or frayed, leaving spaces in between them.

Stressing
Alteration of the natural state of wool fibers through friction while wet or when dry, in order to get the scales of the fibers to open up at the cuticle, giving rise to the felting process.

Superwash
Treatment given to skeins of wool to prevent knitted garments from shrinking when washed in the washing machine.

*T*exture
The order in which fibers are arranged within fabric.

*W*ool
Animal hair used for spinning.

Wrinkling
Irregular folds that occur in fabric when using the nuno felting technique.

Originally published as *Fieltro*
© Copyright ParramonPaidotribo—World Rights
Published by Parramon Paidotribo, S.L.
Badalona, Spain

Managing editor:
María Fernanda Canal

Editor:
Carmen Ramos

Texts:
Elvira López Del Prado Rivas

Execution of exercises:
Elvira López Del Prado Rivas, Mercè Puig,
Cornelia Blüme, Persones llanes,
All you knit is love,
Mª Jesús Fernández

Collection design:
Josep Guasch

Photographs:
Nos & Soto Studio
Elvira López Del Prado Rivas
and artists' own photographs

Layout and page make up:
Estudi Guasch, S.L.

Production director:
Rafael Marfil

Production:
Manel Sánchez

ISBN: 978-84-342-3378-2
Legal Deposit: V-2.917-2008
Printed in Spain